Introduction

In 1954 P&O introduced two new passenger liners to their Australian passenger/cargo service. They were to be the last traditionally designed vessels which the company would build and at almost 30,000 gross tons would be the largest passenger liners operating a regular service 'East of Suez'. The two ships were almost identical in appearance, the main identifying feature being their funnel tops, but, despite their similarity, their careers were to be very different. The *Arcadia,* which was the first of the new sister ships, enjoyed a career which spanned 25 years, during which time she was always a happy and reliable vessel. In contrast to this, the *Iberia's* 18-year life was marred by stability and mechanical problems despite the fact that she was a product of one of the country's most reputable builders.

After just over ten years of service both ships were severely affected by the political troubles in the Middle East, with the subsequent large increases in world oil prices, and by the unassailable competition from air travel. In the late 1960s, as trade on the Australian service fell away, they took increasingly to cruising, a role for which they were ideally suited, unlike the liners built for the North Atlantic.

Both the *Arcadia* and the *Iberia* are still remembered by many people in Europe, North America and Australasia, and I hope that this book will bring back happy memories to all those who were associated with these two handsome ships.

Neil McCart
Cheltenham
September 1993

Jacket Design: Caroline McCart
© Neil McCart/FAN PUBLICATIONS 1993
ISBN 0 9519538 3 4

Typesetting & Printing by
Graphic Print
Springwater House
Taffs Well
Cardiff CF4 7QR

Famous British Liners
ARCADIA & IBERIA

— P&O's Sisters For The 1950s

By Neil McCart

Contents

Published by FAN PUBLICATIONS

17 Wymans Lane, Cheltenham, GL51 9QA, England. 0242 580290

Chapter One

Rebuilding The Fleet

At the end of the Second World War in September 1945, the P&O fleet, like the nation itself, was in a sorry state. The company had lost seven of its passenger ships, four of which had been sunk during 'Operation Torch', the Allied landings in North Africa. So, not only was a heavy rebuilding programme required, but those ships which had survived the war required considerable reconditioning. The war against Japan in the Far East had brought about many political changes in that region, particularly for the European political powers, as the spirit of nationalism made itself felt. Even before the start of the war India had been moving towards some form of self-government, but the traumatic events which followed the Japanese entry into the war and the huge capitulations of British and Commonwealth armies in Malaya and Burma in 1942 and 1943 had made independence for the Indian subcontinent a political reality.

Not least among the factors which affected the P&O company's post-war rebuilding programme was the cost of constructing new tonnage. Prices at the shipyards had risen to over twice those of 1938 and so, in 1946, orders were placed for only two new passenger liners, with two more to follow when economic conditions improved. The orders placed in 1946 were for the *Himalaya* and *Chusan* which were intended for the Australian and Far Eastern routes respectively.

The eleven passenger liners which survived the war had all been requisitioned for government service, and during those years they had been 'hard-used' with long voyages and only the bare minimum of maintenance. Four of the vessels, *Mooltan, Maloja, Chitral* and *Ranchi* dated back to the early 1920s and, once released by the government, they would never return to their original roles. The *Mooltan* and *Maloja* were reconditioned as one-class vessels with berths for 1,030 tourist class passengers apiece. The *Chitral* and the *Ranchi* were refitted in a somewhat austere fashion under the auspices of the Ministry of Transport and, on charter to the Ministry, they carried passengers to Australia under the assisted passage scheme.

Despite these setbacks to trade there were some 'bright spots'. Not only were there thousands of would-be emigrants waiting for assisted passages to Australia, but the passenger liners were the only means of carrying them to the antipodes. The government had lifted its wartime ban on civilian flying on 1 January 1946 and four weeks later BOAC (an amalgamation in 1940 of Imperial Airways and British Airways) had reopened its flying boat service to Singapore. However, for the dozen or so passengers which the *Short Sunderland* flying boats could carry, it was a long and uncomfortable journey. The aircraft flew from Poole in Dorset via Biscarosse, France; Augusta, Sicily; Cairo; Habbariya, Iraq; Bahrain; Calcutta and Rangoon. Soon after this they reopened the London-Sydney service using *Lancastria* aircraft. These were wartime *Lancaster* bombers converted to carry between 12 and 15 passengers (some of them in the former bomb-bays) and the 12,000-mile journey could last between $63\frac{1}{2}$ and 72 hours. Not only was air travel uncomfortable, and something of an ordeal for passengers, but it was very expensive and for the vast majority of travellers well beyond their means.

Throughout the late 1940s experimental work was being carried out on the 'giant' *Bristol Brabazon*, but the news in 1948 that BOAC had incurred an operating loss of £8 million made any threat to the shipping lines from air transport seem very remote.

By 1950 P&O's passenger/cargo trade with Australia had settled down, with the cargo fleet back to its pre-war level and with all the surviving pre-war passenger vessels having resumed their peacetime trade routes. However, the *Mooltan* and *Maloja*, those two beautiful sister ships which had entered service in 1923 and 1924 respectively, were both almost 27 years old. They had been the first P&O passenger ships to exceed 20,000 gross tons and in both their pre-war role, as two-class ships, and their post-war role as one-class tourist ships, they had always been very popular, but the P&O Board under the chairmanship of Sir William Currie had to consider their replacements.

In the years following the Second World War rising inflation dramatically increased the cost of industrial production. The

The P&O liner *Mooltan*, on being released by the government after the Second World War, was reconditioned as a one-class tourist ship. Here she is seen at the Tilbury Landing Stage in 1950. *(FotoFlite)*

shipbuilders and shipowners were not immune from these steep rises in costs and careful thought had to be given to any new building. Against this consideration had to be balanced the vital role which the Merchant Service was playing in the nation's recovery and for P&O it was, as Sir William Currie said: '. . . a question of carrying on or getting out, and the answer was not the latter.'

However, having decided to continue with the shipbuilding programme, there then came the question of who would build the new vessels. Although British shipbuilders were still the 'best in the world', there were now problems with construction as far as passenger ships were concerned. As well as industrial disputes there were difficulties with the supply of steel, and these two factors had caused delivery delays. The shipbuilders themselves were facing the problem of competition from German and Scandinavian shipyards.

Having taken the decision to replace the two 'elderly sisters', P&O's naval architects set to work to design the replacements and, as had always been the case in the past, their size was really limited by the fact that they would have to negotiate the Suez Canal on their round voyages. In the event it was decided that the two new vessels would be similar in appearance and interior design to the *Himalaya* of 1949 but, in the light of experience gained through the operation of that ship, there would be certain modifications. Also, at nearly 30,000 gross tons, they would be somewhat larger. They were to be the last of P&O's traditionally designed mail steamers.

By the early 1950s the *Mooltan* and *Maloja*, which had been built in the 1920s, were outdated and the decision was taken to replace them with two new ships — the *Arcadia* and *Iberia*. *(P&O)*

Chapter Two

The White Sisters

The contracts for the two new ships went to John Brown & Co Ltd of Clydebank and to Harland & Wolff Ltd in Belfast, both of whom were major names in world shipbuilding with a reputation for quality workmanship. The order for the Clydebank vessel, which was to become the *Arcadia,* was placed in the autumn of 1951 and the keel was laid soon afterwards. The order for the second ship, the *Iberia,* followed in the winter of 1951 with the keel being laid in February 1952, by which time the *Arcadia* was beginning to take shape on the stocks.

By the spring of 1953 work was progressing well on both ships and this is how the *Arcadia's* first Chief Officer Mr J. L. Dunkley (later Captain J. L. Dunkley), recalled his initial impressions of the vessel under construction, when she was known as yard number *675:** 'When I arrived at Clydebank in March, *675* had her hull plated to the upper deck (A) and the Promenade Deck beams were just going into place. There were numerous holes in the side for access and for the introduction of machinery, notably a large opening for the stablizer equipment. The shell had been almost covered with coats of priming paints, and when the Queen visited the ship at the time of the launch of the Royal Yacht, *675* was sufficiently covered with white paint to make a brave show. When I went inboard I found the ship was much further advanced in the way of cabin work than I had expected; F Deck cabins were virtually complete with some of E Deck getting on

that way. This state is not unusual and was due, in this case, to the need for keeping the joiner force at work, there being no other ships in the yard on which they could then be employed. There is a vast amount of work for the plumbers in a modern ship and their work, ideally, fits in between the platers', caulkers' etc, and the joiners' and electricians'; but it is difficult to keep this balance and in *675* the joiners had got on faster than the plumbers.'

Mr Dunkley goes on to describe the vast amount of work which had gone into the preparation of plans for the *Arcadia:* 'A water-line model has been built on which to experiment with upper deck arrangements and to get a better idea of how things look than can be obtained from sheets of plans. Of plans themselves, hundreds have been produced showing each space in detail, on a large scale as well as the smaller scale general arrangements, deck by deck. A set of cabins has been built ashore where, over a long period, various fittings, furniture, painting schemes and furnishings have been tested and many changes made to try to achieve the best possible arrangement and colour scheme. A specimen bathroom and shower cubicle has also been made and fittings tried out, even down to ironing board and sleeve board.'

Mr Dunkley considered this was a most useful experience for, as he went on to say: 'In future, when passengers complain about their cabins, I shall be able to tell them something about the work that has been done." The launching date for the *Arcadia* was set for 14 May 1953 and that of the *Iberia* for 21 January 1954, and Mr Dunkley recalls the preparations being made in the spring of 1953 for the great event on Clydebank: 'Another interesting stage reached in April was the building of the launching ways. Before the day of the launch the whole weight of the ship had to be transferred from the blocks and shores, on which it was built, to a cradle on the sliding ways. Underneath the sliding ways are the standing ways, and on these the ship slides into the water. A special gang was engaged on this for many weeks before the launch. There was also shoring up to be done in the ship; in No. 1 hold large baulks of timber were secured criss-cross in the fore part of the hold and vertically above to take the great strain which comes on this part of the ship when the after section becomes water-borne and lifted from the line of the slipway while the fore part is still pressing on the ways.'

Thursday 14 May 1953 was, in fact, a unique day for the British shipbuilding industry for, not only was the *Arcadia* launched on the Clyde, but at Barrow-in-Furness the Orient Line's new 29,000 tonner, the *Orsova,* also took to the water. Both vessels were built for the P&O Group and were to operate a joint service to Australia. At John Brown's yard, Clydebank, the *Arcadia* was named and launched by Mrs D. F. Anderson, the wife of P&O's Vice-Chairman Donald Anderson.** At the luncheon which followed the ceremony Dr J. M. M'Neill, the Deputy Chairman of John Brown & Co Ltd, who presided in the absence of the Chairman, Lord Aberconway, proposed a toast to 'The *Arcadia',* describing her as '. . . the ship of the year, one of the largest, if not the largest, passenger ship building in the world today.' He went on to suggest that she should not be termed a luxury ship because, '. . . she was primarily designed for maximum efficiency and with the most modern equipment to meet competition for many years ahead.'

The keel of the *Arcadia* was laid in the autumn of 1951 and this photograph, taken in January 1952, shows the hull beginning to take shape. A light dusting of snow covers the steelwork. *(P&O)*

*Ships are always known by their 'yard' or 'job' number at the builder's yard, and often these numbers become so familiar to those working on the vessel that they are more easily remembered than the name; the **Queen Mary** was referred to as *534* for many years.

**Later Sir Donald Forsyth Anderson, P&O Chairman 1960-1971.

On Thursday 14 May 1953, watched by the work-force of John Brown & Co Ltd, the *Arcadia* thunders down the slipway into the River Clyde. *(P&O)*

Sir William Currie, the Chairman of P&O, in his reply pointed out how he saw that day: 'The occasion is unique in two respects. One is that two of the famous family of Anderson have each launched a great ship on the one day and within a few hours. The other is that in one day two companies closely related have put in the water 58,000 tons of shipping for the services of Britain and the Commonwealth.' He also pointed out two particularly notable features in connection with the design of the *Arcadia* — the special precautions taken to ensure the quality and purity of the fresh water which would be used on board, and the dimensions and shape of the funnel, which had been designed to reduce the problem of smoke and soot deposits to a minimum. The 'Clydebank' funnel of the *Arcadia* would become her most easily identifiable feature and its shape was the outcome of useful team-work between P&O's technical representatives, the Thermo-tank Company of Govan, and the builders.

As the launch party left the yard later that afternoon, tugs towed yard number *675*, now officially the *Arcadia*, to John Brown's fitting-out berth.

The *Arcadia* takes to the water for the first time. She was launched by Mrs D. F. Anderson, the wife of the P&O's Vice-Chairman. *(P&O)*

At Belfast the *Iberia's* hull takes shape as steel plating is fitted to the Promenade Deck. *(Harland & Wolff)*

Eight months later, at noon on Thursday 21 January 1954, yard number *1476* was ready to be launched from Number 12 slipway in the Musgrave Yard of Harland & Wolff Ltd at Belfast. A graphic account of the ceremony has been left by the vessel's first Chief Officer, Mr W. N. Eade (later Captain W. N. Eade): 'The naming ceremony was performed by Lady McGrigor, wife of the First Sea Lord, Admiral of the Fleet Sir Rhoderick McGrigor, who was also present. In addition to the large number of guests, a considerable crowd of shipyard employees and their friends gathered to witness the launch of this fine ship, one of the largest passenger vessels built at Belfast since the war.

About 20 minutes before the actual time of the launch, guests began to assemble on the launching platform, a large construction which had been made for the occasion. From this high vantage point, only a short distance from the stem, one was able to observe the great bows of the ship and to appreciate her beautiful lines. Looking at the bow cradles and launching ways which supported the whole weight, it seemed amazing that this massive, towering vessel, of a total weight of 14,840 tons, remained resting as she did and that shortly she would slide down the ways into the water.

An apprentice from the yard presented Lady McGrigor with a bouquet before she ascended the platform, and a short but most impressive religious service preceded the launch. This consisted of a prayer, followed by a portion of the 107th Psalm, which was read by the Rev. J. H. Carson, of Westbourne Presbyterian Church, Belfast. On the stroke of noon eight bells rang out and Lady McGrigor performed the naming ceremony and started the *Iberia* on her run to the water.

Slowly but surely this great white ship began to move down the slipway, and as she gathered speed there was a loud and prolonged cheer from the onlookers. As the bows left the slipway and the whole ship became water-borne, her way carried her some little distance before the drag wires took the strain and checked her. Tugs then took control and towed her to a berth in another part of the yard for fitting out.'

'Slowly but surely this great white ship began to move down the slipway.' The *Iberia* was launched on 21 January 1954. *(Harland & Wolff)*

In the speeches which followed the ceremony there were ominous references by Sir Frederick Rebbeck, the Chairman of Harland & Wolff, who spoke of the growing foreign competition for British shipbuilders and the steady decline in orders. Today, when one considers the precarious state of the shipbuilding industry, Sir Frederick's fears seem well justified.

However, such gloomy thoughts could not mar the joy and excitement at the respective launching ceremonies which had taken place on the Clyde and at Belfast. The names which had been chosen for the two ships, Arcadia and Iberia, went back to P&O's early days. In the 1830s the first Iberia was recorded as being, 'the finest ship afloat.' She was a wooden-hulled paddle-steamer of 516 gross tons which served the company's route from London to Gibraltar, via Lisbon and Oporto. In 1844 she carried the novelist William Makepeace Thackeray on a Mediterranean cruise and four years later, in 1848, she sailed under secret Admiralty orders from Southampton to Cherbourg to evacuate refugees fleeing from political revolution in France. The Arcadia also had one predecessor in the P&O fleet, a 6,000-ton steamship employed for much of her service, between 1888 and 1914, on the Bombay route.

In the early 1950s it seemed that the Arcadia and Iberia had a career of 30 years, at least, ahead of them.

Everything is in place for the launch of the *Iberia* as her huge hull towers over the launching platform.

(Harland & Wolff)

Chapter Three

Comfort Not Luxury

At over 29,500 gross tons, and with an overall length of almost 719ft, the two P&O liners were the largest passenger vessels built for the British merchant fleet during the 1950s and, apart from the *Caronia,* they were the biggest liners to be built between 1945 and 1960. With their curved, rounded stems, cruiser sterns, two masts, a single elliptical funnel each and rounded bridge fronts they were handsome vessels whose graceful lines and attractive appearance were much appreciated in the maritime world. Both were instantly recognizable by their unique funnel designs, the *Arcadia* with her dome-shaped 'Clydebank' funnel and the *Iberia* with a 'coaming', which disguised what would have been a somewhat peculiar appearance.

The design of the passenger facilities took account of the changes in post-war trade and, although there was accommodation for 670 first class and 730 tourist passengers on the most up-to-date lines, the emphasis was on comfort rather than luxury.

There were some differences in the style of the various public rooms on board the two ships, but the layout was basically the same and so a full description of the *Arcadia's* accommodation will suffice. On both ships the first class passengers were housed on the Boat Deck, the Promenade Deck, then down through A, B, C, and D Decks in well-appointed single-, two- and three-berth cabins. On A Deck there was a variety of rooms which offered single-berth cabins with showers or baths, two-berth cabins with either private or shared facilities and four, three-berth rooms with shared bathrooms. Amidships on B Deck there were eight special de luxe cabins fitted with retractable beds so that each room could be converted, as required, to a sitting-room. The rooms were also intercommunicating, so that, if desired, private suites could be made available. All eight of these staterooms were fully air-conditioned, as were all the inboard first class cabins on both ships.

Most of the first class public rooms were situated on the Promenade Deck and they were described at the time as being, 'colourful and decorative, but not ultra-modern in style.' The dining saloons were situated on D Deck, but the most interesting room in both the *Arcadia* and the *Iberia* was the Observation Lounge which was situated at the forward end of the Boat Deck, immediately below the navigating bridge. Large windows were set into the bulkheads on three sides of the room, and comfortable armchairs, with foot-rests, were placed so that their occupants looked outboard. On the after bulkhead there was a bar counter. In the *Arcadia* this counter was decorated on either side with a representation of a ship's figurehead,

The most interesting room in both ships was the Observation Lounge at the forward end of the Boat Deck. In this view of the *Arcadia's* Observation Lounge the bar counter decoration of a ship's figurehead can be seen.
(Author's collection)

The *Arcadia's* first class library on the Promenade Deck. It was open to the main foyer, screened only by a pillared and balustraded barrier. *(Author's collection)*

The *Arcadia's* first class lounge, showing the central section and, at the far end, the mural which featured an 'Arcadian' scene. *(Author's collection)*

based on actual models fitted to old sailing ships. On a central table in the *Arcadia* there were terrestrial and celestial globes, while the deck-covering carried a design featuring maps of the two hemispheres. In the *Iberia* the lounge was fitted with a chart-table, gyro-compass repeater and other navigational recording instruments. These rooms were unique in vessels which were engaged on the Australian trade route and needless to say, they were very popular with passengers.

The first class children's nursery was placed well forward on the Promenade Deck and in the *Arcadia* it was fitted with a central room-divider which enabled the hostess to separate children of different ages. The walls were lined with plastic which was decorated with amusing motifs by Miss Margaret Gilbert.

Aft of the nursery, and separated from it by a stretch of open deck which formed the children's playground, were the library and writing rooms. The library was situated centrally and was open to the main

The *Arcadia's* first class swimming-pool, which was aft of the Verandah Café. *(Author's collection)*

foyer, screened only by a pillared and balustraded barrier in the *Arcadia,* and glass panels decorated with pot plants in the *Iberia*. Casement windows at the forward end overlooked the children's playground and these were screened to provide privacy. At the sides of the room there were glass-fronted bookcases and the furniture consisted of shaped built-in divan seats, settees and easy chairs. At each side of the library were writing rooms with both forward and side-facing casement windows. In the *Arcadia* the furnishings were in shades of lichen and moss green, with contrasting gold, orange and beige. In the evenings the full curtaining at the windows provided a wonderful expanse of colour in a contemporary design. The furniture, of sycamore and walnut, included single and double writing desks, with occasional tables and chairs.

Aft of the foyer, port and starboard passageways led to the wide

entrance doors of the lounge. In both vessels this was a large room, with windows on either side. In the *Arcadia* the central section of the ceiling was circular in shape (and elliptical in the *Iberia*), with a panelled perimeter, all arranged to carry concealed lighting for general illumination. One of the most interesting features of the *Arcadia's* lounge was seen at the forward end, where three sides of a deep recess, formed between the porches of the two entrance doors, were panelled in low relief, each panel carrying an inlaid motif of a single classical subject. Another focal point was at the after end where, between the glazed doors which led to the dance floor, there was a wide, deep mural painted on a concave section of panelling and featuring an 'Arcadian' scene.

Immediately aft of the lounge was the dance space which was enclosed on both sides by folding glass screens with the musicians' platform at the forward end between the two entrances. At the after end, doors on either side led to the Verandah Café, which served as the main bar and smoking room. Two wide bay windows, with

The *Arcadia's* first class Verandah Café, which served as the main bar and smoking room, with the decorative panel which represented a chart of the world. *(Author's collection)*

panelled and pillared surrounds, were the outstanding features of the room, and a central bar faced forward towards a decorative panel representing a chart of the world. The main panelling of the room was in vertical figured olive ash and bird's-eye maple, with a teak trim. The bar counter also served the pool café, which was divided from the Verandah Café by decorated glazed screens. Two plastic panels on the bar front in the pool café depicted scenes on the Grand Canal at Venice taken from paintings by R. M. D. Robertson.

The first class dining saloon on D Deck was entered from the foyer through revolving doors on either side which, if necessary, could be folded away to leave clear entrances. The saloon occupied the full width of the ship and it was almost 100ft in length. Seating accommodation was provided for 366 passengers at tables for two,

The *Arcadia's* first class Promenade Deck, looking aft on the starboard side. *(Author's collection)*

four or six, and a raised central section enhanced the sense of spaciousness. The panelling in the compartment was in veneered hardwoods of walnut and sycamore, with figured woods such as English cherry being used extensively.

On the starboard side of A Deck, aft of the cabin accommodation, both ships were provided with a purpose-built cinema which was an innovation on P&O liners. The first class swimming-pool was situated on the Promenade Deck, aft of the pool café, and it was surrounded and sheltered on both sides by the changing rooms.

The tourist class passengers in both vessels were accommodated on the Promenade Deck, A, B, C, D, E, and F Decks. The two-, four- and six-berth cabins were situated on D, E and F Decks with the public rooms on A, B, and C Decks. The gallery, which was equipped with a bar, was located on the port side of A Deck and aft of this came the shop and hairdressing salon. On B Deck, aft of the Bureau, was the dance floor which occupied virtually the full width of the ship and which was enclosed by folding glass screens, as in the first class

The *Iberia's* first class Observation Lounge was not as ornately decorated as that of her sister ship.   *(Author's collection)*

equivalent. At the forward end there was a platform for the band, while the after-end bar also served the Verandah Café, which was entered through glass doors aft and by wide screens from the open deck. This room was decorated with light-coloured veneers of zebrano and ash and pale grey-green leather-covered panels. In the centre of the room there were curved alcoves into which were fitted built-in divan seats.

Aft of the Verandah Café was the children's nursery which, like that in the first class, was panelled in plastic and decorated with roundels showing native Australian birds and animals. The lounge and smoking room were both on C Deck, with the former at the forward end. Large casement windows at both sides looked out over the weather-deck to the open sea. The panelling was in figured French birch, with contrasting elm, whilst the windows were framed

The tourist class Verandah Café on board the *Arcadia*. It was situated on B Deck, aft of the dance space.   *(Author's collection)*

The *Arcadia's* first class dining saloon on D Deck.   *(Author's collection)*

with sycamore, and decorative marquetry inlays were set into the cupboard fronts and the sides of the central casing. Aft of the lounge was the tourist class Smoking Room which was furnished in light grey, powder blue and ivory. The chairs were upholstered in leather, and this material was also used in feature panels which were set into the bulkheads.

The tourist class dining saloon was on D Deck aft of the first class saloon and separated from it by the galley, bakery and other food preparation areas. Seating was for 376 passengers at tables for four, six and eight, and the room was panelled in figured willow, relieved by designs in quilted turquoise-coloured leather.

Points of general interest which were common to the first and tourist classes on both the *Arcadia* and the *Iberia* were the extensive use of fluorescent units for concealed illumination, and the wide use of 'Formica' plastic panelling.

Not only were the first class de luxe and inner cabins air-conditioned, but so too were the dining saloons for both classes,

The first class lounge in the *Iberia*, showing its elliptical central section and the concealed lighting.   *(Author's collection)*

the first class hospital and, to the relief of the purser's office, the Bureau on B Deck aft.

In order to comply with the requirements of the Ministry of Transport in the 1950s, the accommodation for the crew of 711 was of a high standard with both the European stewards' messroom, which was forward on B Deck, and that of the Goan stewards, which was amidships on the starboard side of E Deck, being air-conditioned.

As well as just over 1,400 passengers, the two liners were able to carry large quantities of both general and insulated cargo in six cargo holds, three forward and three aft of the machinery spaces. The six hatchways were served by 16, 3-ton and two, 10-ton tubular steel derricks which were controlled by 18 electric cargo winches.

The company decided to fit both vessels with a two-shaft arrangement of Parsons triple casing, geared steam turbines designed for a total normal ahead power of 34,000 SHP, and an overload power of 42,000 SHP, with propeller revolutions of 130 and 140 per minute, respectively. Each HP ahead turbine was of the impulse-reaction type having two rows of impulse blades, followed by 29 rows of reaction blading. In each IP ahead turbine there were 35 rows of reaction blading and in each LP ahead casing, which were of the double-flow type, there were eleven rows of reaction blading in each half.

The astern turbines were comprised of a three-row impulse wheel incorporated in each IP ahead casing and a three-row impulse wheel in each LP ahead casing. When running astern the turbines were capable of developing 22,000 SHP.

The gearing for the ahead turbines was double-reduction type, the primary gears being enclosed in a fabricated steel gear case which was independent of the main gearing. The gearing for the IP and LP ahead turbines was of the single-reduction type.

Steam was supplied to the turbines by three Foster Wheeler, oil-fired, controlled superheat, water-tube boilers. The superheater outlet pressure was 530 psi with a temperature of 850°F. Each boiler was provided with an economiser and a regenerative air pre-heater and fitted with both forced- and induced-draught fans. This main propulsion machinery was designed to give the two ships a service speed of 22½ knots.

Electrical power for operating most of the auxiliary machinery, as well as for the rest of the ship's requirements, was provided in both vessels by three self-contained turbo-generators, which were manufactured by the British Thomson-Houston Company of Rugby. Each set was capable of delivering 1,200kW at 225 volts DC, and each had its own condenser, closed-feed control valve, air ejector and extraction pump. The generators were driven by turbines, which took steam directly from the main boilers, at 5,500 rpm, which was then reduced to 600 rpm through single-reduction gearing.

As regards life-saving appliances, both vessels were equipped with 18 lifeboats, which included two class 'A' motor lifeboats, four passenger motor lifeboats, ten 'Fleming'-type lifeboats, four oar-propelled lifeboats and two accident lifeboats, all constructed in aluminium alloy and stowed under 'Welin-Maclachlan' gravity davits. However, whilst cruising, specially built launches, which were nicknamed 'limousines', were fitted.

As the Christmas and New Year festivities of 1953/54 drew to a close, the first of these magnificent new ships was nearing completion.

The tourist class lounge in the *Arcadia*.   *(Author's collection)*

The *Iberia's* tourist class Verandah Café, showing the murals which depicted rural life in the Iberian penisular.   *(Mrs M. Dykes)*

The *Iberia's* tourist class dining saloon which was on D Deck. *(Mrs M. Dykes)*

Chapter Four

East To The Antipodes

The first of the two sisters to be handed over to the P&O Company and to depart on her maiden voyage was the *Arcadia*, but not before she had been involved in two minor mishaps, which some of the more superstitiously minded might have interpreted as unlucky omens for the future. The first incident happened on Monday 21 December 1953 as the *Arcadia* lay in 'Brown's Basin' at the company's Clydebank shipyard, with most of the fitting-out work already completed and only four weeks to go until her official trials. This particular day had been set aside for the launching of the 10,936-ton Federal Steam Navigation Company's general cargo ship MV *Essex,* and unfortunately, the weather conditions on the Clyde were very unsettled at the time. As the *Essex* became water-borne, a gale-force gust of wind caught her and before the tugs were able to take control, she was swept upstream and her bow collided with the *Arcadia's* stern. It was fortunate that neither ship sustained serious damage, mainly scraped paintwork and dents which did not delay the *Arcadia's* completion.

A newspaper correspondent who visited the *Arcadia* during that month described the scene thus: '. . . everything on board was in that state of well-ordered confusion which is the despair of the unititiated but the delight of the architect who sees his planning becoming reality. Bunches of wires were hanging from ceilings and threatening to lasso the unwary walker. Massive vans on the wharf had brought furnishings from all parts of the country, and as workmen were putting the finishing touches to various items, P&O stewards were carrying chairs, tables and carpets — all the items required in the final furnishing of the great liner. Here and there a heavy wooden stairway was in use, but ready to make way for the permanent structure.'

It is difficult to convey adequately all that is involved in fitting out a great liner, but at sea both the *Arcadia* and the *Iberia* were communities of over 2,000 people, stocked with all that was required to maintain them for a period of at least four weeks of voyaging, with reserve supplies to meet emergencies. There were more than 1,000 cabins to be equipped with beds, dressing-tables, wardrobes, chests of drawers, wash-basins, cabinets, carpets and lighting. Bedding alone amounted to 14,000 sheets, with a similar number of pillowcases, and 5,000 blankets. In addition there were the public rooms to be furnished in appropriate style to cater for the differing tastes of the first and tourist class passengers. However, by the end of December 1953 steam was up on the main boilers and smoke could be seen curling from what had already become known as the 'Clydebank' funnel.

Another milestone in the P&O Company's history passed almost unnoticed on Thursday 7 January 1954, when the elderly *Mooltan* arrived at Tilbury Landing Stage on completion of her final voyage from Australia. As her passengers streamed ashore her Asian crew boarded trains for Glasgow where they would join the *Arcadia*. For the *Mooltan* the only prospect was the shipbreaker's yard, and as she steamed north to Faslane she passed Belfast Lough during the

The *Arcadia*, having successfully completed her trials, arrived at Tilbury Docks early on the morning of 2 February 1954. Here she is seen about to negotiate the entrance lock. *(Museum of London)*

afternoon of 21 January where, only a few hours before, the *Iberia* had been launched and where, 31 years previously, she herself had first entered the water.

On Wednesday 20 January 1954 the *Arcadia* was able to leave Clydebank under her own power, and steam south to the Gladstone Dock in Liverpool for dry docking. Once there her stabilizer fins were fitted and the underwater hull was painted. After four days at Liverpool she steamed north once again on 26 January to begin her official trials on the Clyde. These included speed runs over the Arran measured mile and during these trials her mean speed over the nautical mile was 24.7 knots, more than two knots faster than her designed service speed. Her Third Officer, John Blackburn, also recalls that she was delivered to the company with the funnel dome painted buff, as was the rest of the funnel but, 'It was found necessary to continually wash it clean of soot and so this was rapidly abandoned and the dome was painted black, with a modicum of varnish to give it a shine.'

Despite the fact that the finishing touches still had to be made in fitting out the passenger accommodation and 150 of John Brown's employees had to remain on board to finish the work, the *Arcadia* was officially handed over to the P&O Company on Saturday 30 January 1954 at a small ceremony which was carried out after she had anchored off the Tail of the Bank. The P&O Chairman, Sir William Currie, took delivery and Captain Geoffrey C. Forrest RD RNR took command of the new liner. Captain Forrest had first joined the P&O Company in 1914, just before the outbreak of the First World War, and after service as an RNR officer during that war, he was appointed Fourth Officer of the *Kalyan* in 1919.

He served in the *Borda* and the *Delta*, before being appointed Chief Officer in the *Rajputana* in 1935. After further RNR service between 1939 and 1945, he rejoined the company and became the Staff Captain on the *Strathnaver*. Following this he commanded the *Canton, Chitral* and the *Stratheden*, before being appointed to the *Arcadia*. Mr Michael J. Miles, who was an Assistant Purser with the company remembers him well: 'Commodore Forrest was a gentleman who was much respected by all who knew him. He was ever mindful of the welfare of his crew and he had his own small dinghy stowed on the after end of the bridge, which he used to sail himself when conditions at various ports permitted. When cruising, and indeed at ports *en route* to the antipodes, where the ship had to anchor off, Commodore Forrest often arranged for a pontoon to be towed to a nearby beach and, in order that off-duty crew members could enjoy a swim, he arranged for lifeboats to ferry them to and from the ship. On occasions Commodore Forrest would accompany them and if it was a particularly hot day he would be seen gently swimming with a white sunhat on his rather balding head.'

The inaugural voyage from the Clyde to Tilbury was something of a 'trial cruise' as she embarked 300 guests, among them the Minister of Transport, Mr A. T. Lennox-Boyd. The *Arcadia* left the Clyde during the evening of 30 January and 24 hours later she put in to Tor Bay for the night. The following day she steamed along the south coast and that evening Sir William Currie hosted a dinner on board in the first class dining saloon. He was able to read out a number of congratulatory telegrams, including one from the Chairman of the Cunard Steamship Company. He also expressed his appreciation of the achievement by John Brown & Co in, '. . . delivering a beautiful ship in time for her to begin her maiden voyage to Australia on 22 February.' He went on to say, 'tongue in cheek', that by their

The *Arcadia*, with her 'Clydebank' funnel dome now painted black, arrives in Sydney for the first time on 28 March 1954. *(P&O)*

During the summer of 1954 work progressed on fitting out the *Iberia*. In the background Shaw Savill's *Southern Cross* is also being fitted out. *(Harland & Wolff)*

completion of the liner the Clydebank company had enabled him to win a modest bet with Mr A. E. Anderson, Chairman of the Orient Line, that the *Arcadia* would be completed before the *Orsova* — both vessels having been launched on the same day. (*Orsova* was handed over on 10 March 1954).

After spending most of Monday 1 February at anchor off Portland, the *Arcadia* headed for the Thames and entered Tilbury Docks early the next morning. Two days later, as she lay alongside No. 32 Shed with John Brown's electricians and joiners completing their work on board, smoke was seen billowing from the starboard side of the first class Verandah Café and the fire alarms were sounded. Fire parties were immediately mustered and fortunately they were able to confine the outbreak to the cork insulation around some steam pipes, and it was quickly extinguished. The smoke blackening was soon

cleared up and work could continue to prepare the vessel for sea.

Happily there were no other serious problems, and on the afternoon of Monday 22 February 1954 the *Arcadia* was able to leave Tilbury Landing Stage for her maiden voyage to Sydney. It was a cold, grey day, but a little colour was added to the river scene that day with the ship dressed overall. A crowd of well-wishers gathered on the Landing Stage and the media gave the event good coverage with the BBC interviewing Captain Forrest personally. The Third Officer on the voyage was John Blackburn who recalls that: 'Despite all the senior officers being RNR, the Red Ensign was flown and we dressed the ship overall at each port. I spliced an extra set of flags onto curtain rings for speed of hoisting and lowering at 8.00 am and sunset respectively.' The *Arcadia* was fully booked for the voyage and amongst her first class passengers was the P&O Chairman, Sir

William Currie. The ship reached Port Said on 1 March and Sir William and Lady Currie held a cocktail party there for the Governor of the Canal Zone, Mr Mohamed Riad. After an overnight transit of the canal, the *Arcadia* left Port Suez the following day and called at Aden three days later. It was during that week that the air-conditioning, limited though it was by today's standards, was much appreciated by the first class passengers. The *Arcadia* arrived in Sydney on 28 March 1954 for a six-day stop-over, and the ship was much acclaimed by the Press and media. She returned home by the same route, calling at Melbourne, Adelaide, Fremantle, Colombo, Bombay, Aden and Port Said, arriving at Tilbury on the morning of 6 May 1954.

For that summer the P&O Company had organized an extensive programme of 14 UK cruises, five by the *Chusan* and nine by the *Arcadia*. Apart from the initial cruise, which started in London, all the voyages commenced at Southampton and the first three were 13-night cruises to Mediterranean ports. In early July the *Arcadia* made an eight-day cruise to Lisbon and Casablanca, followed by another of 13 nights to the Mediterranean. The highlight of that season was a three-week cruise which took her to Greenock (for the first time since her acceptance trials), Bergen, Oslo, Gothenburg, Hamburg and Amsterdam, before returning to Southampton early on the morning of 20 August. On 11 August, while cruising from Bergen to Oslo, the *Arcadia* passed through Karm Sound, the northern part of which forms Haugesund Harbour. About two miles south of Haugesund, a fishing town, the channel narrows to about 200 yards in width and on board the *Arcadia* the cheers and whistles of children lining the shore could be clearly heard. At that point a road bridge was under construction and the *Arcadia* was one of the last large ships to navigate the channel before the two halves were joined, barring the passage of the big liners. After another two cruises into the Mediterranean and one to the Atlantic Islands, the *Arcadia* returned to London on 14 October 1954 to prepare for her second Australian voyage 12 days later. During that summer she had been 'shown off' to most of Europe and everyone had been most impressed.

Mr Michael J. Miles also recalls that Commodore Forrest was: 'One of the first "close coasters" when, for the benefit of passengers on both line voyages and cruises, he would take the *Arcadia* as close to the shore as possible. Passengers were very appreciative of this and, in the days before the "Broadway" style entertainments, it kept them interested and happy.'

Meanwhile, in Belfast, the work-force at Harland & Wolff's yard had not been idle, and during the summer of 1954 work progressed on fitting out the *Iberia*. One of P&O's management staff, Mr John Church, visited her at Belfast on the last day of July that year and he has left his 'layman's' memories of the visit: 'My first glimpse of the *Iberia* was from a starboard window of the aircraft as we came down to land. Even from that height, and amid the murk and gloom of the evening, the ship's white hull and high buff funnel stood out boldly against the background of Queen's Island. It was my first visit to a shipyard and I went down to *Iberia* at her fitting-out berth at the Victoria Yard the next morning. My first impressions were of incompleteness and a bewildering confusion. Perhaps it was the absence of the ship's boats, revealing a jagged row of empty davits, that contributed most to her unfinished external appearance. But there was plenty of other evidence; scores of workmen were visible, ashore and on board, wheeling up loads of piping, ventilation trunking and other fittings, hoisting them aboard, welding, hammering, painting with an activity that seemed, yet could not be, quite uncoordinated.

When we went on board these impressions were not at once dispelled. We picked our way along alley-ways, through public rooms and across open decks, climbing over or under trestles, gingerly holding aside festoons of doubtfully insulated temporary electric cables, sidling past men working every few feet along our path. There were hundreds of men; men laying deck planking, caulking it, and then smoothing it over with a machine that looked comically like a lawn-mower; men working over the dizzy depths of lift shafts; men finishing terrazzo floors in the galley; men fixing panelling, light fittings, furniture; men painting, welding, hammering.

We spent a too-short hour and a half touring most of the passenger accommodation, with glances at the Asian crew's quarters and the refrigerated stores. Mr Davis, the *Iberia's* Deputy Purser, was particularly pleased with these — their shining surfaces of Kynal plate would be easy to keep clean and hygienic. But in all our journey we did not see a room or space that was wholly completed — except for the tourist class cabins on F Deck, which were locked. Some parts of the ship were far advanced; the dining saloons needed a little more installation of their decorative panels and the placing of furniture. But other sections were barely recognizable, and it was very difficult to visualize how the ship could be ready to sail for her trials in little more than a month's time. However, Mr Davis said that progress had been quick enough up to then, and it was impossible to come away unconvinced by the serene confidence of all concerned that she would be finished in good time and be a very fine vessel indeed.'

Fortunately Mr Church's fears were groundless and on the evening of Tuesday 7 September 1954 the *Iberia* left Belfast for her preliminary trials. After carrying out various tests, on Saturday 11 September she underwent speed trials on the measured mile at Arran, during which she achieved a mean speed of 24.9 knots which, as with the *Arcadia*, was well above the required service speed of 22.5 knots. That afternoon a small ceremony was held round the first class swimming-pool on the Promenade Deck, when Sir William Currie accepted delivery of the *Iberia* and Captain C. E. Pollitt RD* RNR took command. After service in the RNR as a midshipman during the First World War, Captain Pollitt had joined the P&O Company in 1919. From 1937 to 1944 he served in the *Strathaird* as First and then Chief Officer. After the Second World War he had commanded the *Mooltan*, *Strathaird*, *Strathmore* and *Strathnaver*, before being appointed to the *Iberia*.

After completing her delivery voyage from the Clyde, the *Iberia* arrived at Tilbury on the morning of Monday 13 September 1954, and just over two weeks later, on Tuesday 28 September, she left London for Australia. Once again the berths were fully booked and it was 10 December that year before she returned to London.

The first voyage of the *Iberia* is recalled by Derek Orchard of Victoria, Australia, who was a Senior Lounge Steward on board: 'After a very rough and uncomfortable night crossing on the Irish Sea ferry I joined the *Iberia* about two weeks before we sailed for trials. To my dismay the ship was in a state of chaos with workmen crawling all over her, but we sailed on time with a complement of travel agents, photographers and company officials. During the trials cigars, cigarettes, and all kinds of wines and spirits were freely available which, for many, made for a very impressive measured mile.

When we left Tilbury for the maiden voyage there were still workmen on board, but the disruption to passenger amenities was kept to a minimum. The six first class lounge stewards had come from various ships of the fleet where the floor coverings in public rooms was the usual linoleum, and the thick pile carpet in the *Iberia's* lounge caused us to develop enormous blisters on our feet. Fortunately a change of footwear from foam rubber to plain leather soles eased our discomfort. I can also recall that in the first few days, when the weather was cool and all the lounge windows were closed, the room became fogged with thick cigar smoke. After dinner coffee was served in the lounge and the passengers crowded into the compartment, making the thick blue haze almost unbearable to us all.

Amongst the passengers on that voyage were six people who did the round trip. There were two elderly maiden ladies, a retired insurance director and Lord and Lady Harlech. Most days they congregated at the forward part of the lounge, under the tapestry,

Arcadia at Cape Town in December 1956.   *(Don Smith)*

The *Arcadia* berthed at Southampton on 6 May 1976, having returned from a three-week Caribbean cruise.   *(Don Smith)*

and they kept this position for most of the voyage. Needless to say this area soon became known as the "royal box".

I can recall that in Colombo an "illegal" passenger came on board and made a home in one of the very broad lampshades which graced the lounge. Its main diet was flies and it had a voracious appetite but, upon our arrival in Fremantle, I took a very contented praying mantis ashore and released it.

In all I served in the *Iberia* for two years, including a season of cruises to Scandinavia and the Mediterranean. The work was long and hard compared to the *Canton* and the *Strathaird* but, as far as I was concerned, she was a happy ship.'

P&O now had seven large passenger liners serving the route to Australia, with the *Arcadia* and *Iberia* ranked as the most important ships on that major trade route.

September 1954 and the *Iberia* lies in Tilbury Docks shortly before sailing on her maiden voyage to Australia.

(Museum of London)

Chapter Five

Collision At Sea

On Christmas Eve 1954 the *Iberia* left London for Sydney with 1,200 passengers, and during the afternoon of Friday 31 December she arrived in Port Said for what should have been a routine 24-hour transit of the Suez Canal. However, Captain Pollitt was told that the canal was blocked and that his ship would be delayed indefinitely. At 3 am that morning the Liberian-registered oil-tanker *World Peace* (10,892 gross tons), which was fully laden and on passage from Kuwait to Gibraltar, had suffered a steering gear failure and collided with the El Ferdan railway bridge, midway between Kantara and Ismailia. The bridge, which was constructed during the Second World War, was an important link as it carried the strategic railway between Egypt and Palestine. After the collision, the *World Peace* passed sideways between the two spans of the railway bridge and the after end of her deck fouled one side of the western span. This part of the span then jammed up against the superstructure of the tanker and was lifted off its pedestal and carried forward until the other end became embedded in the bank of the canal. The tanker then swung round and went aground with her bows stuck in the canal's western bank. Because of the great danger of fire breaking out, all her crew and those in the vicinity of the bridge were evacuated. Seven other ships, including four laden tankers which had been steaming behind the *World Peace*, were moved away to a safe distance and the canal company's engineers brought a 150-ton floating crane to raise the bridge span which had been wedged onto the tanker's deck.

The unexpected build-up of shipping at Port Said brought a welcome boost to trade for the shopkeepers and caterers of Port Said, but the delay was frustrating for the seamen concerned. Captain Pollitt himself takes up the story: 'I went by road the following day (Saturday 1 January 1955) to El Ferdan to see the damage and what I saw was certainly an amazing sight. There was the tanker, aground forward, her stern in the middle of the canal with one end of the bridge resting on her after deck and the other end embedded in the bank of the canal. However, the canal engineers were already busy with their preparations to clear the canal. Their plan was to place a pontoon beneath the bridge, and close to the ship. This pontoon was then to be partially sunk and a platform built on it to reach to the underneath side of the bridge. The water was then to be pumped out of the pontoon until the platform took the weight of the bridge. The bridge was then to be cut in two close to the ship, thus freeing the vessel.

In due course all this was done and the ship hauled clear. The remainder of the bridge was then cut up into three pieces and dumped onto the side of the canal by floating cranes.

By the morning of 3 January there was a ship in almost every berth in Port Said harbour and ships were still arriving. To relieve the

The *Iberia* at sea during the 1950s. This aerial view shows her open decks to their best advantage. *(FotoFlite)*

A damaged section of the *Iberia's* Promenade Deck is cut away by the staff of Cockatoo Dockyard, Sydney, following her collision with the *Stanvac Pretoria. (Author's collection)*

congestion, all the southbound ships that were waiting were moved into the canal and made fast. I got as far as Kantara where I remained for 24 hours. That night the canal was declared clear for the passage of ships and the southbound vessels began to move at 7 am on the morning of 4 January; a very long line of ships, of which I was the forty-sixth.

The plan was to pass all the southbound ships through first and then pass through all the northbound vessels that were waiting in the Bitter Lakes and at Suez. I arrived at Suez on the evening of the 4th, having been delayed for three days.'

The *Iberia* had been the largest ship involved in the hold-up and arrangements were made for excursions from Port Said to Cairo and Luxor, which 150 passengers took advantage of. Special arrangements had to be made with the British Consul in Port Said to obtain 'temporary' passports for the assisted passage families, who did not normally require them.

Fortunately, at that time of the year few of the canal's pilots were away on leave and there were 150 available to help clear the backlog of shipping. The *Iberia* eventually arrived in Sydney on 27 January 1955, three days late.

After making one more Australian voyage, the *Iberia* began a summer season of six cruises from Southampton, starting on 11 June 1955, and she was joined by the *Arcadia* a few weeks later on 16 July. The *Iberia's* programme included the Atlantic Isles and the Mediterranean, as well as a 13-day cruise to the Fjords calling at Oslo and, on the return leg, Amsterdam. In the autumn of that year both vessels returned to the Australian mail service and enjoyed trouble-free sailings for the next few months. The *Iberia* was in the news when an Australian dockers' strike forced her to return to England with thousands of tons of British exports still on board, including cars, machinery and textiles. But in the spring of 1956 she was involved in a very serious incident.

Repairs are made to the *Iberia's* damaged port side, April 1956.

(Author's collection)

The *Iberia* returns to Tilbury after a voyage to Australia.

(Museum of London)

The *Iberia* left Tilbury Landing Stage for Sydney, with 1,300 passengers on board, during the afternoon of Wednesday 14 March 1956. On 19 March she called at Navarino Bay (now Kiparissia) on the west coast of Greece to embark emigrants bound for Australia, of whom there were thousands in those days. She reached Port Said two days later on 21 March and made her southbound transit of the Suez Canal that night. During the afternoon of Saturday 24 March she moored off Steamer Point in Aden, where she remained until early the next day when she left for Colombo. Up to that point there had been nothing untoward about the voyage.

She had been due to dock in Colombo at 8.30 am on Thursday 29 March, for a stay of about 12 hours, during which time refuelling would be carried out and her passengers would be able to go on sightseeing trips to Mount Lavinia and Kandy.

However, during the evening of 28 March, when she was about 100 miles south-west of Cape Comorin, she encountered some extremely rough weather with high winds and heavy seas. At about 1.30 am the next morning she was still ploughing through high seas and she was about 170 miles off Colombo when, suddenly, the whole ship shuddered violently from stem to stern for several minutes. Some passengers were thrown from their bunks and some in the tourist class, who were sleeping on camp beds on the upper decks in order to escape the heat, not only felt the violent collision and shuddering, but heard the crash and grinding of metal as the bows of an empty oil-tanker ploughed into the port side of the *Iberia's* Boat Deck abaft No. 10 and 12 lifeboats. Suddenly there was a great cacophony as the vessel's sirens boomed, alarm bells sounded and emergency doors were slammed shut. Fortunately there were no serious injuries and all the passengers were soon at their emergency stations and the situation could be assessed.

It was evident that the *Iberia* had been rammed broadside on by the 10,201 gross ton, Panamanian-registered oil-tanker *Stanvac Pretoria*, which had left Tanjung Uban in Indonesia on 24 March for the Persian Gulf. Luckily she had been in ballast at the time of the collision and it was her stem and forepeak which had inflicted the damage on the *Iberia's* Promenade and Boat Decks. Damage to the tanker was confined to the shell plating and to two store-rooms in the forepeak, and she was able to make for Bombay to undergo temporary repairs.

On board the *Iberia* there was some concern that the port side of the Boat Deck, which had been set down by about three feet, would collapse altogether and so the passengers berthed on that side of the ship were ordered to remain in the public rooms as the vessel set course, once again, for Colombo, but at a much reduced speed. She finally arrived in the port at 2.30 pm on 29 March and temporary repairs were put in hand. The surveyor's report of the damage to the *Iberia* ran thus: 'Boat Deck port side, set down by approximately three feet maximum, about 80ft long, in way of No. 10 and 12 lifeboats. The Promenade Deck set down, maximum 11ft, about 80ft long and deck pillars in way crumpled. A Deck set down slightly at outer edge for 80ft and deck pillars crumpled. Shell plates 10 and 11 port side aft at common seam indented slightly over eight frames.' As a temporary measure, shoring was erected on A Deck and the Promenade Deck and repairs were carried out to ensure that the launching davits for boats 10 and 12 were serviceable.

As the passengers were treated to weekend excursions into the heart of Ceylon (Sri Lanka), conferences were taking place to determine the quickest way of getting the ship back into normal service, with the least inconvenience to the passengers. An early decision was taken to cancel the first of the *Iberia's* summer cruises

The *Arcadia* at Tilbury Landing Stage in the mid-1950s.
(Museum of London)

from the UK which had been due to begin on 2 June 1956, but it was hoped that repair work could be executed in time for the ship's second cruise on 23 June and so avoid disappointing hundreds of passengers. It was quite obvious that extensive repairs would have to be effected and it was decided that Cockatoo Dockyard in Sydney offered the best opportunity of getting the vessel back on schedule in the shortest possible time. So at 6.30 pm on the evening of Monday 2 April, with the port side of the Boat Deck, A Deck and the Promenade Deck still roped off and 'out of bounds', she left Colombo to continue her voyage to Sydney.

Proceeding at a moderate speed, the *Iberia* arrived at Fremantle on 9 April and was met by the Shipyard Superintendent of the Cockatoo Dockyard, the Senior Ship Surveyor to Lloyd's and senior directors of MacDonald, Hamilton & Co, who would be able to make authoritative decisions on the spot. During the time the vessel was at Fremantle the situation was assessed and dimensional sketches of the damaged steel decks were prepared so that prefabrication could begin immediately. The Shipyard Superintendent and his assistants returned to Sydney by air and started work on the preparation of the steel for the damaged decks. Four days later, on her arrival at Melbourne, a working party from Cockatoo Docks met the ship and during the remainder of the voyage they carried out all the labelling and marking of the decks, fittings and deckheads. Whilst the ship was in Melbourne, lifeboats No. 10 and 12 were lifted from their davits and landed on the tourist class sports deck. The two davits were cut away and placed temporarily on a floating crane, the intention being to load them on to some other part of the ship. However, before this could be done, a strong wind blew up and the crane was ordered away, so the BI liner *Chyebassa* took them on to Sydney instead.

The *Iberia* finally arrived in Sydney on Monday 16 April and as soon as disembarkation had been completed the liner was taken into dockyard hands. Because so much preparatory work had already been done, the repairs could be started within two hours of tying up, and the work continued on a 24-hour basis, seven days a week until the ship was ready for sea again.

By 26 April 1956 the replacement of all the steel plating to the Boat Deck, Promenade and A Deck had been completed and the wooden deck planking could be laid. The boat davits had been put back and work was under way to repair the port high pressure turbine. The surveyor had found that the reaction blading was quite extensively damaged, with the impulse blading not so badly affected.

Seven weeks after having arrived at the port with extensive damage to her port side, the *Iberia* was as good as new once again, and on Saturday 5 May she left Sydney to return to England via the Australian ports, then Colombo, Bombay, Suez, Marseilles and

Gibraltar, arriving at Tilbury Landing Stage on 8 June 1956. She started her first summer cruise from Southampton to Santa Margherita and Madeira as scheduled on 23 June that year and, fortunately, the remainder of the year passed without any serious incident.

For the *Arcadia* events were far less traumatic and between 25 October 1955 and 19 June 1956 she made three round voyages between London and Sydney, all via Suez. As Michael Miles recalls: 'The *Arcadia*, being the commodore ship of the P&O fleet, enjoyed her share of celebrities who travelled regularly. I can recall Sir Robert Menzies travelling with us twice and I had the privilege of taking him ashore in one of the four "limousine" lifeboats which the *Arcadia* carried. It was Commodore Forrest's idea that Assistant Pursers should be taught to handle these lifeboats and, having achieved my degree of proficiency, I took Sir Robert ashore in Malta, from where he flew to London for a conference. He was a very interesting man and he once kept the Purser, the Deputy Purser and me up until about 2.00 am regaling us with stories of Australian and international politics which were absolutely fascinating.'

On 30 June 1956 the *Arcadia* also started her European cruise programme, but the political situation in the Middle East was deteriorating, and this caused the cancellation of some calls in the eastern Mediterranean. By the autumn of that year when the two ships were back on the Australian passenger service, the whole route east had been changed.

The *Arcadia* at anchor in Colombo Harbour in the mid-1950s. *(N. W. Pound)*

Chapter Six

The Cape Route

The year 1956 was a particularly difficult one for Britain with momentous events taking place in the nation's foreign affairs. That summer the *Arcadia* and *Iberia* carried out a full cruise programme, which included visiting the Mediterranean but, ominously, some of the eastern ports in that area had been removed from the cruise itineraries. The cause was, from the British point of view, the Suez Canal.

Since its opening in 1869, successive British governments had kept a firm grip on this strategic waterway, for it was a vulnerable thread in the Imperial sea lanes and the route to India. The British government owned 40% of the Suez Canal Company's shares and the defence of the canal had been a British responsibility, with a garrison having been stationed in the Canal Zone since 1882. In 1914, when Turkey entered the First World War on the German side, Britain had declared a 'Protectorate' over Egypt and although Egypt was declared 'independent' in 1922, Britain continued to maintain large garrisons of troops in the country.

However, after World War Two, Britain's role on the world stage began to decline and Egyptian nationalism was becoming a force to be reckoned with. Under a treaty of 1936, Britain had been granted the right to maintain up to 10,000 troops in the Canal Zone and this treaty was due to expire in 1957. The Egyptians, however, were not prepared to wait for the expiry of what they considered to be an unfair treaty, and in October 1951 they abrogated it. In July 1954, after acrimonious negotiations, it was agreed that British troops would leave the Canal Zone within 20 months, but the bases would be maintained for reoccupation in the event of an attack on Egypt. In

June 1956, not only did the last British troops leave Suez, but the strong nationalist army officer who had organized the coup against the corrupt government of King Farouk in 1952, Gamel Abdel Nasser, became the President of Egypt.

It is quite natural and right that the Egyptians should have control of the Suez Canal and the revenues which were earned by it, and had the question of ownership been approached in a calm and balanced way, then an agreement which was acceptable to all the parties concerned could have been reached. Unfortunately in Britain Nasser, who did a great deal of good for his people, became 'Public Enemy Number One' while the Egyptians viewed this 'British Colonialism' with hatred. When, on 26 July 1956, President Nasser nationalized the Suez Canal it set the stage for one of the biggest military and political fiascos of modern history — an attempt by the British and French to take control of the Suez Canal by force.

The reaction in both London and Paris to Nasser's proclamation was one of expected militancy, and amid involved and complicated international diplomacy, preparations were put in hand for a military operation against Egypt. It was only then that the full extent of unpreparedness of both Britain and France to carry out the undertaking was revealed.

During July and August 1956 as the British and French military build-up based on Cyprus ground on, both the *Arcadia* and *Iberia* cruised into the Mediterranean, but neither vessel travelled any further east than Venice. Oddly enough, the Suez Canal continued to function as it always had done with ships passing through in both directions, despite the Suez Canal Company ordering 500 of its

The *Arcadia* in the Suez Canal.

(P&O)

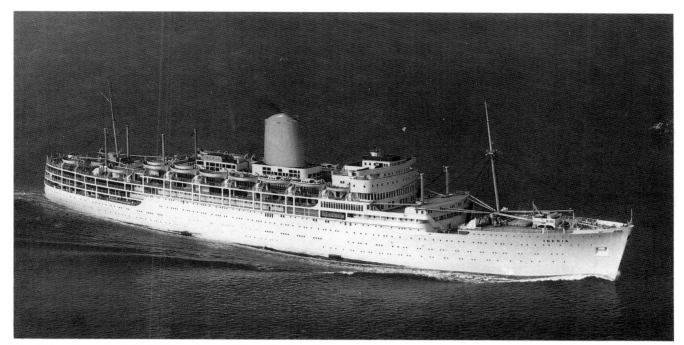

The *Iberia* under way in the English Channel, outward-bound for Australia.   *(FotoFlite)*

non-Egyptian employees to cease work — a move which halved the manpower of the canal pilots. As the weeks went by, the possibility that the British and French would take military action seemed increasingly remote. However, when the *Iberia* returned to the Australian route on 27 September 1956, she sailed via Las Palmas and Cape Town, calling at the two ports on 30 September and 9 October respectively. She arrived in Fremantle on 20 October and Adelaide three days later, as the *Arcadia* left London for Sydney via the same route.

On the last weekend in October 1956 British and French troop convoys put to sea for what were said to be 'large-scale exercises in war conditions' and a day or so later on Monday 29 October the Israelis launched a massive attack against Egypt, across the Sinai Desert. The British and French assault started on 31 October 1956, ostensibly to 'protect' the Suez Canal from the warring countries and keep the waterway open, but in fact it was a clumsy attempt to reoccupy the Suez Canal Zone. For Britain and France 'Operation Musketeer' ended ignominiously in December 1956, by which time the Suez Canal had been well and truly blocked by 27 scuttled ships in the region between Port Said and Suez. The Egyptians had also blown up the El Ferdan railway bridge and a pontoon bridge at the southern end of Lake Timsah. The United Nations clearing up operations would take four months, so it would be a long time before the Suez route was used again.

The autumn and winter months of 1956/57 saw the familiar shipping lanes through the Red Sea and Indian Ocean deserted and so too was the normally much-frequented Mediterranean Sea with mainly troop transports in evidence between Gibraltar and the eastern Mediterranean. The P&O liners had to plough long courses over the vast expanses of the Atlantic and Indian Oceans, with four and five thousand miles at a stretch, and hardly a sight of land, becoming commonplace. For many of the ships' officers memories of long wartime voyages were evoked, although without the discomforts and perils of those years. One former passenger, Richard Greenwood of Swansea, recalls just such a voyage in the *Iberia*, sailing from Sydney for London on 3 November 1956: '*Iberia* cast off promptly at noon, streamers floating from the ship's side, and with a nostalgic chorus of the "Maori Farewell" the ship steamed sedately out of the lovely Sydney Harbour and past the Heads into the

steady swell of the Tasman Sea. The voyage was the more adventurous as our two young daughters were with us and the steward kindly brought a cot for our two-year-old, before bringing us tea. A busy evening followed with an evening meal at 5.30 pm in the children's dining-room, our own descent to dinner being at 8pm. The following day brought us to the Bass Strait and we followed the coastal liner *Westralia* through the shallow waters of Port Phillip to dock at Melbourne, across the jetty from the *Orcades*. A three-day stop was scheduled here and we made a daily journey on the antiquated suburban train to Flinders Street Station.

A 10 pm departure from Melbourne (7 Nov) was followed by a three-day crossing of the Great Australian Bight, with cloudy skies, a steady head wind and a long swell, through which *Iberia* pitched with a strangely rapid motion. The daily routine was now established, with the two nurseries in long rooms just forward of the superstructure. One for the under-sixes in charge of a somewhat formidable, but not unkindly Scots nurse; and the other for the six-to 12-year-olds, with a younger and more genial nurse. The early evening was the most difficult part of the day when we had to turn

Iberia berthed at Tilbury Docks at the end of a long voyage.

(Museum of London)

23

the cabin lights down to allow the youngsters to get ready for sleep, and at the same time dress for dinner in a small cabin which was even more limited for space by the cot.

It was at this stage of the voyage that the ship's itinerary was confirmed. The 1956 "Suez" crisis was at a critical period; the canal was closed, a UN force was being organized and the Soviet Union was intervening in Hungary. We were not sorry to learn that the *Iberia* was to be re-routed by way of Cape Town.

Arrival at Fremantle was at 7 am on Remembrance Sunday (11 November) and we had only four hours ashore. With shops and cafés closed we went on a bus tour, which included the lovely King's Park. Nine full days at sea followed and our route to Cape Town, which was plotted on a chart in the ship's foyer, was a straight line on the map, extending for 4,928 nautical miles. The bearing of our course never varied significantly and we averaged 510 nautical miles a day at an average speed of 21 knots and, travelling west, we gained 20 minutes each day. I asked the First Officer why our track did not lie further southward in order to gain some advantage from a small circle course, but he explained that any reduction in mileage from a more southerly track would be outweighed by stronger head winds and greater discomfort to passengers.

For the most part, this leg of the voyage was not particularly rough, but there was an acute awareness of a sense of isolation for we saw not a ship, not a bird, not even a fish in the Southern Ocean. The days, however, passed pleasantly enough. Formal meals were leisurely affairs, faultlessly served by attentive Goan waiters and afternoon tea in the lounge, to the accompaniment of the ship's orchestra, was greatly enjoyed. In the afternoon too, the nurses brought their charges on deck for games and competitions and the mothers' egg and spoon races, and fathers' three-legged races caused mild excitement. Of course swimming and deck games passed the time when the weather was good and when it wasn't, there were the lounges and bars and the library. It is interesting that, although the *Iberia* carried approximately equal numbers of first and tourist class passengers, there was no contact of any kind between the two groups. Indeed, each class appeared to be completely unaware of the other's existence.

With persistent head winds, the sheltered parts of the open decks were in great demand and on days eight and nine the speed was reduced to ensure a timely arrival at Cape Town. Awaiting the pilot in Table Bay, Table Mountain and the Lion's Head looked remote in the early morning mist, and a variety of ships were queuing up for the pilot; we followed the *Uganda* which was *en route* to Mombasa. During our day at Cape Town (21 November) we went on a bus tour to Fish Hoek, returning by way of the Wynberg vineyards.

The voyage north from Cape Town was altogether delightful. After the Cape rollers were left behind, the sea was calm, water and sky were blue and the evenings on deck balmy. A variety of ships passed us southbound and signals were exchanged with P&O's *Corfu* and *Strathnaver*. By day silver flying fishes skimmed the water and we

Iberia passes the Needles as she steams out of The Solent.　　　　　　　　　　　　　　*(FotoFlite)*

The *Arcadia* in the River Thames.

(A. Duncan)

saw schools of dolphins, and at night the constellations "Orion", "Cassiopeia" and the "Plough" climbed even higher in the sky. Open-air activity was at its peak, culminating in a boisterous "crossing the line" ceremony around the swimming-pool. Children and adults each had their own fancy dress party and the tropical gala dinner was a splendid occasion. However, after the sultry weather of the tropics, Las Palmas (30 November), provided a welcome port of call.

The last three days passed quickly, with passengers impatient to be ashore. The sea became steadily rougher, the sky cloudier, the wind more boisterous and the *Iberia* resumed her rapid pitching movement. We were now in the "northern winter" and early one morning the Devon coast appeared out of the early morning mist. As the pilot came aboard off Brixham, shafts of sunlight shone on the hills, and as we moved up Channel the air grew colder. The Thames was shrouded in fog — we were home.

Even the grim journey on the slow, crowded boat train could not dim our happy memories of a delightful voyage in the *Iberia*.'

The New Year of 1957 saw the *Arcadia* at Tilbury Docks after completing a voyage from Australia during which she received a severe buffeting in the Bay of Biscay. The liner had been caught by storm force winds and mountainous seas which, at one stage, caused her to heel over by about 40°. Michael Miles recalls the voyage: 'At the end of December 1956 we were on our way home from Australia by way of Cape Town. Towards the end of the voyage we were crossing the Bay of Biscay when we encountered a tremendous storm. Unfortunately the stabilizers had broken down earlier in the voyage and at one stage the ship was rolling 40° to both port and starboard. Over 400 pieces of furniture were damaged, including the piano in the tourist class lounge which broke loose from its "moorings" and it took several crew members to secure it. Waves also broke over the after end of the ship and cascaded down through the tourist lounge, causing considerable damage. First sitting at dinner that evening got soup and the second sitting got nothing at all. At about 9.15 pm I was asked to make a broadcast to all the passengers asking them, in the interests of safety, to retire to their cabins. However, many didn't and they congregated in the lounges where they assisted the crew to strap down the furniture. They then sat on the decks of the public rooms watching the violent storm outside.' That night, in order to give the passengers a chance to

sleep, the *Arcadia* hove to and, luckily, by the following morning the storm was beginning to die down. When the liner docked at Tilbury on New Year's Eve she was only a few hours late.

One passenger on the voyage, Mr Mervyn Shaw of Dublin, said that he was flung across the lounge into a table, and furniture and other passengers piled up about him. People found it impossible to walk upright and, '. . . we had to crawl along on our hands and knees. Some of the passengers were near to panic, but the stewards had done very well in calming everyone down.' Captain E. R. Bodley, who was completing his first voyage as Commodore of the P&O fleet commented: 'It was a short and severe winter gale, with heavy seas, and I think the *Arcadia* took it well. The wind came from the worst possible direction for us and we had to steam slowly into the heavy seas, an exceedingly tricky operation. We were steaming like this for nearly eleven hours. It was the worst storm I have seen in the Bay of Biscay for 36 years and it certainly shook up the passengers.'

On her next return voyage from Australia, which was again via Cape Town, the *Iberia* left Fremantle for London on 4 February 1957 and, after only a few hours at sea, she was forced to put back with engine trouble. Upon inspection it was found that the white metal of several bearings had fused, and repairs took four days before she was able to continue her voyage. She arrived home on 3 March 1957 and made only one more round voyage to Sydney via the Cape and Durban, before starting her summer cruise season from Southampton.

During 1957 the *Arcadia* made two voyages to Australia by way of Southern Africa. On the first of these she called at only Las Palmas and Durban, before crossing the southern Indian Ocean for Fremantle. She started her summer cruise schedule from London on 29 June 1957 and made five cruises, including three weeks round the North European Capitals and two long Mediterranean cruises.

The Suez Canal was finally declared clear on 7 May 1957 and the first of the two sisters to use the waterway once again was the *Iberia*. She left London for Sydney on 24 September that year and after calling at Vigo she made her transit of the canal on 1 October 1957. She was followed from London by the *Arcadia* on 22 October 1957 and she completed her southbound transit between Port Said and Suez eight days later, on 30 October. The two ships were again able to use the shorter and traditional route to Australia.

Chapter Seven

On Into The Pacific

The late 1950s were good years for all the P&O liners, and particularly for the *Arcadia* and the *Iberia* which were still the pride of the fleet, with the *Canberra* not yet in service. Both vessels continued to make voyages to Australia with 'Ten Pound Migrants' filling the tourist class berths, albeit in somewhat declining numbers now, while the first class passengers still favoured the liner voyage over air travel. Cruising was, as always, extremely popular and there were no 'package holidays' to lure potential cruise passengers away.

In the summer of 1957 Mrs Margaret Dykes of Doncaster took a three-week Atlantic cruise in the *Iberia*, '. . . at the magnificent price of £90 in a tourist class four-berth cabin. In the diary which we

received at the end of the voyage it states that the ship stopped at 3 am on 22 June, for a lifeboat to be sent away to embark a patient from the British tanker *Stanwell*. However, what is not mentioned is the disappearance overboard of a crew member. It was the afternoon of 23 June, before we arrived at Bermuda, when those of us who were up on deck noticed that we had changed course and that the ship appeared to be turning back. We all wondered why, but nothing was said over the loudspeakers and it wasn't until that evening when a brief announcement was made that we knew what had happened. That night searchlights from the bridge scanned a wide area of water on both sides of the ship but, despite shouts of "there he is" from watching passengers as they mistook "white horses" on the waves

An unusual view of the *Arcadia* and *Iberia* together off the Isle of Wight on 15 August 1959. Both ships were outward-bound on Mediterranean cruises.

(FotoFlite)

Another view of the sisters together off the Isle of Wight on 15 August 1959.   *(FotoFlite)*

for the missing crewman, nothing was found. We were young then and the tragedy was not taken as seriously as we would see it today and there was a lot of speculation about a late arrival in Bermuda. We never found out why the crew member had "jumped", but, of course, rumours were rife.*

At the time a three-week cruise to Bermuda was the height of luxury, yet, by today's standards, the facilities in the *Iberia* were very primitive. We didn't have a cinema, but a screen was put up on deck and canvas stacking-chairs set out for the audience. This depended on the weather of course. Even the menus which, at the time, we thought exotic, look quite simple today when compared with those on the *Canberra*.'

Mrs Pamela Bowen of Hampshire recalls a cruise she took with her parents: 'In July 1957 we embarked on the *Iberia* at Southampton for a cruise to Venice and Malaga. Once we were at sea the days took on a lively pattern with activities such as aqua-sports and various deck games. Each passenger was made to feel especially welcome and I well remember my first experience of choppy seas and the movement of the ship. The cabin steward, realizing my distress, found me a sheltered corner up on deck and brought me beef tea. After this I made a rapid recovery and later that day I enjoyed afternoon tea.

Sunbathing soon became possible and there were cocktail parties, as well as wonderful meals served by attentive Goan waiters. I particularly remember the delicious curries for which P&O is famous.

I will never forget our arrival in Venice, very early on a hot, sunny morning. A number of passengers rushed on deck to watch our entry through the many islands to the anchorage close to the quayside and St Mark's Square. It was delightful to be able to gaze down on the gondolas which were carrying flowers to the hotels of the city.

Upon departure from Venice we set course for Malaga, once again enjoying all the shipboard activities. In the evenings there were fancy dress parades and "dog racing", all supervised by Captain Pollitt and his officers. For me, one of the highlights of the cruise was a birthday party which was arranged by the entertainments officer and which proved to be a memorable evening. It was with some sadness that we all disembarked in Southampton, with our souvenirs and very happy memories of life on board a P&O liner.'

At a stockholders' luncheon on board the *Arcadia*, which Sir William Currie hosted on 21 October 1957, he was able to read out a letter which he had received from one satisfied passenger: 'One may feel a legitimate pride in this great achievement of British skill and enterprise, and I must confess to a thrill as I think of her carrying our flag to far distant lands and not apologising for it either.' He went on to tell his audience how the *Arcadia* had just completed five cruises during which she had carried 5,486 passengers, and that the next day she would depart for India, Ceylon and Australia with 1,345 passengers on board. Unfortunately this voyage was disrupted by dockers taking industrial action in the Australian ports, resulting in the *Arcadia* falling three days behind schedule. In order to make up one of those days for her passengers, they were disembarked at Southampton on the last day of December 1957, instead of at Tilbury the next day. With the delivery of Britannia 102 aircraft to BOAC that year it was becoming even more important to keep to published timetables.

In January 1959 P&O announced that both the *Arcadia* and the *Iberia* were to make cruises from Sydney to New Zealand, into the Pacific Ocean and to ports on the West Coast of the USA in November 1959 and January 1960 respectively. It was announced that the *Arcadia* was to be taken out of service, '. . . on completion of her present voyage in March', in order that she could be fitted throughout with air-conditioning. It was clear that P&O intended the two vessels to have a 'modern' image when cruising in US waters.

In February 1959, whilst on a voyage home to London from Sydney, the *Iberia* was northbound in the Suez Canal during the evening of 15 February when, at 71Km, she ran aground with her bow stuck in the mud. Fortunately she was refloated under her own power and she arrived at Port Said at 1.20 am the next morning, where divers examined the underwater hull and found it to be

*The member of the ship's company concerned was Assistant Cook Eric Dyson of Morecambe, Lancashire.

undamaged. She left the port at 8.15 am that day, none the worse for the incident, but having held up both the north and southbound convoys.

The *Arcadia* arrived back in London on 22 March 1959 and after disembarking her passengers and destoring she left Tilbury for Harland & Wolff's Belfast shipyard, arriving alongside her berth at Thompson Wharf on 1 April. As well as having full air-conditioning fitted, 170 of her first class cabins were to be given private shower and toilet facilities, which would reduce her passenger capacity in that class from 679 to 657. 275, or 42 per cent, would then have private facilities. It was also intended that the tourist class cabins would be refurbished during the refit.

A week after the *Arcadia* had arrived in Belfast, on Tuesday 7 April 1959, normal nightshift work was being carried out when a fire was discovered at 11.45 pm in the after section of the ship. Within minutes the stern was enveloped in smoke, but the alarm was raised and the ship's fire-fighting teams quickly went into action. They were soon joined by Harland & Wolff's fire force and at just after midnight the Belfast Fire Brigade was summoned. The outbreak was traced to the after hold where replacement furniture was being stored and where workmen had been earlier in the day. Because of toxic fumes from burning plastics, the firemen had to wear breathing apparatus and work in relays, but by 2 am on 8 April the blaze had been brought under control and then quickly extinguished.

After what was, in effect, only a minor set-back, the work on the *Arcadia* was completed well ahead of schedule, and on 11 June 1959 Sir William Currie held a dinner on board for the officials and foremen

of Harland & Wolff, to show his appreciation. In his speech Sir William thanked everyone for the 'expeditious' work which they had performed on the *Arcadia*, '. . . enabling her to keep to her summer cruising programme.' He also spoke about the 'new' ship *Canberra* which was on the stocks nearby. The *Arcadia* left Belfast the next day, Friday 12 June 1959, commanded by Captain Geoffrey A. Wild who, in 16 months' time, would be appointed as *Canberra's* first master. After an overnight trip from Belfast to the Mersey, the *Arcadia* embarked 400 guests in Liverpool for the two-day journey to Tilbury, where she was to start her summer UK cruise season.

Meanwhile, in May 1959, the *Iberia* left London for a 24-day cruise across the Atlantic to Tenerife, Havana and New York. It was new ground for P&O, and although they would not visit the Cuban port again, they would become a familiar sight in US waters.

Having completed five Mediterranean cruises, the highlight of the season for the *Arcadia* was a three-week Atlantic cruise calling at Lisbon, New York and Bermuda. She left Southampton at 1 pm on 12 September 1959 and berthed in Lisbon two days later for a stay of just over 23 hours. Then after a five-day Atlantic crossing, during which she steamed at reduced speed through gale force winds and heavy seas, she arrived off the Ambrose Light Vessel at 12.53 pm on 21 September and embarked the New York Harbour pilot. It was the *Arcadia's* first call at a US port and the city of New York laid on one of its traditional welcomes with fire-boats, helicopters and harbour craft all taking part. At 3.15 pm that day the *Arcadia* berthed at Pier 90 on West 50th Street for a two-day stay.

She sailed for Southampton again at 5 pm on 23 September,

The *Arcadia* in Southampton Docks in the late 1950s.

(Southampton City Museums)

The *Iberia* at Vancouver in October 1960. *(J. K. Byass)*

arriving back early on the morning of 3 October after steaming some 7,785 nautical miles during the three-week cruise. It had been a great success with her passengers, and once they had disembarked, she left Southampton for Tilbury that same day, for this was the last of her summer cruises and the next voyage would take her to Sydney via Suez, then on into the Pacific as part of a new P&O service. At the company's annual general meeting earlier in the year, Sir William Currie had announced that: 'The Orient & Pacific Lines service is being extended from the Pacific ports of North America to Japan and the East. We have great hopes for the future of tourism in the Pacific. There has been a remarkable increase in travel through the area in the last five years, the bulk of which originates in America.' And so the *Arcadia* left London on 20 October 1959 for an absence from UK waters of just over four months. She made the traditional passage calling at Port Said, Aden, Bombay, Colombo and the Australian ports, before arriving at Sydney on 20 November. Two days later she left on a cruise to Hobart, Wellington and Auckland, before returning to Sydney on 6 December. While docking at Auckland she struck the wharf which damaged the shell plating and set in two scuttles. On 11 December she left Sydney for a 40-day cruise around the Pacific and the West Coast of the USA, making her first call at San Francisco on 30 December. She sailed again the following day and on New Year's Day 1960 she was at Los Angeles, after which she steamed west into the Pacific again, bound for Suva. On 20 January 1960 she returned to Sydney and the cruise was voted a resounding success, in spite of a 15-hour delay in Suva when a wire fouled her port propeller, and despite the fact that she sank a wooden barge while approaching her Pyrmont berth in Sydney. Three days later she left for London once again sailing via Colombo and Suez. However, when she was 24 hours out of Port Said, speed was reduced because of engine trouble and she was a day late arriving back at Tilbury.

Meanwhile the *Iberia* had followed her sister ship to Sydney in December 1959, and she too crossed the Pacific during February and March 1960 and made calls at the US West Coast ports. From Los Angeles she made a return visit to Honolulu and from there she sailed north-west to Yokohama, Kobe and Hong Kong. She returned to London via Manila, Singapore, Colombo and Suez — the usual route taken by P&O's Far Eastern liners. In early October 1960, to cater for the increasing number of US cruise passengers, it was decided to call the *Arcadia's* dining saloons 'restaurants'. Accordingly the first class saloon was renamed the Olympic Restaurant, whilst that in the tourist class became the Corinthian Restaurant.

On 19 October the *Arcadia* left London once more for what had become, by then, an almost routine four-month voyage. The winter was spent cruising in the Pacific Ocean with calls at the US West Coast ports over the New Year. Early on the morning of Thursday 5 January 1961 the *Arcadia*, with 1,895 cruise passengers aboard, was approaching the harbour at Honolulu, where she was to spend 12 hours. The pilot had been embarked and the weather was fine and sunny with a calm sea, when the liner struck a coral reef 300 yards off the harbour entrance and went aground, bow first. Although she took a list of four degrees, it was not thought necessary to disembark her passengers, and despite attempts to refloat the ship under her own power, the *Arcadia* remained stuck fast for over two hours until, at 9.30 am, she was freed with the assistance of eight tugs. After she had berthed, divers were sent down to survey the damage, but fortunately this was limited to small indentations in her keel plates and she was able to continue her voyage to Auckland and Sydney. An enquiry into the incident found that the blame lay with the Honolulu pilot, who was subsequently suspended from duty for two months.

However, despite these mishaps, both the *Arcadia* and the *Iberia* enjoyed great success with their operations in this area.

The *Arcadia* in the Arabian Sea, outward-bound for Australia, having just left Bombay on 3 November 1960. *(N. McCart)*

Chapter Eight

Challenge From The Air

On 13 January 1961 the *Iberia* left London for Southampton where she was to undergo a modernization refit at Thorneycrofts, costing P&O £500,000. She arrived at No. 40 berth in the Eastern Docks the next day and the work began immediately, the main feature being the installation of an air-conditioning plant to serve the whole ship. All the passenger and crew accommodation was to be refurbished, which included fitting showers and toilets in 100 first class cabins, and a complete survey of all the main propulsion machinery, propeller shafts and boilers was to be carried out. The whole refit lasted for 70 days, after which the liner returned to London, sailing ten days later for Sydney and the Pacific. Captain C. Barry Thompson was her Chief Officer at the time and he recalls this particular voyage: 'My next passenger ship was the *Iberia* and although she was not a happy ship, nor one which I look back on with any great affection she, I suppose, holds a special place in my heart in that it was whilst serving in her that I met my wife Diana. She was travelling back to New Zealand and I met her at the tourist class cocktail party. I was appointed as Chief Officer of the *Iberia* refitting in Southampton and we departed on 27 March 1961 for Tilbury. We left Tilbury on the first fully air-conditioned voyage on 6 April 1961, going out via Gibraltar, Port Said, Aden, Colombo, Fremantle, Adelaide, Melbourne and Sydney. We had a week in Sydney and during that time I continued to court Diana. From Sydney onwards we had the interesting and unusual experience of being chartered, almost fully, by the Rotary Clubs of Australia and New Zealand who were travelling by sea to an international conference in Tokyo. The voyage got off to a good start because all these Rotarians

A splendid port side view of the *Arcadia* dressed overall. *(Author's collection)*

either knew one another or, in the spirit of Rotary, very quickly got together. Leaving Auckland, where Diana disembarked, we went on to Suva and then straight to Yokohama, where we had nine days whilst the Rotarians attended their conference. From Yokohama we went to Kobe, Nagasaki, down to Hong Kong and to Manila, where we had an incident where a politician was refused entry to the ship because he did not have a pass. This caused a furore and we were refused clearance to leave the port until the captain went ashore and formally apologised for this "insult".

Our homeward voyage from Sydney was billed as a "Safari Voyage" and from Fremantle we went to Mauritius, Zanzibar and then up to Aden, the Suez Canal, Piraeus, Naples, Lisbon and returned to London on 6 August 1961. Ten days later we started the summer cruising season until 6 October, when we left Southampton for London. We left again on 17 October 1961 for a typical P&O voyage as far as Auckland where, naturally, I was delighted to see Diana again. We had a problem leaving Auckland, with salt in our boilers, and we hadn't even got clear of the port when there was a complete electrical failure, and we had to return for five days until the damage was rectified. We sailed again on 30 November for Suva, Honolulu, across to Acapulco in Mexico, through the Panama Canal, Balboa, Cristobal, Curacao, Trinidad, Lisbon and back to London on New Year's Eve. I left the *Iberia* in early January 1962, because my mother was very ill and I did not go back to that ship. The *Iberia* was a very difficult vessel to operate and from a Chief Officer's point of view she was a headache. She had a stability problem, and we could never produce enough water to provide for the passengers on the long trans-Pacific voyages, and this meant occasional rationing, which does not go down very well with first class passengers. We also had the stability problem — the ship simply lacked stability. In Sydney, on one of the homeward voyages, we loaded several hundred tons of zinc ingots in the bottom of the lower holds to assist stability. I understand that this actually "cost" P&O money. Strangely, she was a sister to the *Arcadia* which was always a happy and successful ship.'

The problems with the *Iberia's* stability were very real as Captain C. R. Short recalls: 'The difference between the two ships' relative stability was also very marked, the *Iberia* being much less stable. She was a "seven-day" ship, whilst the *Arcadia* was a "nine-day" vessel. This meant that the *Iberia* could only travel for seven days between ports before having to bunker in order to maintain a positive stability. If this was not possible then the fuel oil tanks had to be "salted up" with sea water ballast, with the inherent problem of cleaning them

The *Iberia* afloat in dry dock at Southampton.　　　*(M. Beckett)*

before oil could be bunkered again. I have a frighteningly true story which illustrates the *Iberia's* "Achilles heel". I can recall that we were once steaming along with a one degree list to port, with the stabilizers in full operation. However, whenever possible, it was always preferable to have the fins retracted as they reduced our speed by half a knot. The controls were on the port side of the chartroom and the commodore asked me to switch off the gyro control, which I did. However, whilst I made my way over to the list indicator which was amidships, the ship started to heel over to port alarmingly and it was increasing in momentum. By the time I got back over to the control box and switched on the gyro again the list had reached 18° and she was still heeling over fast. Fortunately she eventually steadied at 28° and started to return to the upright. I do not wish to over-dramatize the situation, but I am perfectly sure in my own mind that had I not turned on the gyro controls once again, the ship would have "turned-turtle" and we would have been one more "disaster at sea" statistic. It was obvious that the fins were holding the unstable ship upright.'

In October 1961, during one of her Pacific cruises, the *Arcadia* called at Seattle where, being the first P&O passenger ship and the largest liner ever to call at the port, she was given a colourful welcome typifying the Pacific Northwest. However, when she was leaving the Tilbury Landing Stage for Sydney and whilst turning in Gravesend Reach, she struck the quayside, damaging her stem. She then dropped and dragged her anchor, the cable of which became fouled in the Gravesend Upper Ship Buoy, causing further damage to her stem. However, two hours later she anchored and at midnight she came back alongside the Tilbury Landing Stage. After a survey it was decided that the damage was not serious and she was able to leave the port the next day, Christmas Eve.

By the early 1960s the competition from the airline companies was very real indeed. The Boeing 707 had now entered service and the offer, in 1962, to passengers who wished to visit Australia, to travel one way by sea and the other way by air, showed that this threat to the liner's domination of the route to Sydney was being taken seriously by P&O. The *Arcadia* and *Iberia* were not yet ten years old, but suddenly the future did not seem to be so secure. The *Iberia*, in particular, would be beset by mechanical problems.

The *Iberia* left London for Sydney and the Pacific on 4 August 1962, and she reached Port Said, as scheduled, seven days later. However, on Sunday 12 August, after having completed her southbound transit of the Suez Canal, she struck a sandbank near Port Tewfik at the southern entrance to the canal. It was clear from the ensuing vibration that the port propeller had been damaged, but she was able to continue her voyage to Sydney at reduced speed. Upon her arrival there she was dry docked and an inspection revealed that the blades of the port propeller had been bent backwards by about 15 inches. Fortunately the shaft itself was undamaged, so a spare propeller was soon fitted and the *Iberia* could get back on schedule. In February 1963 it was the *Arcadia's* turn to suffer delays. She had left Sydney for London on 19 January, and the voyage had been a routine affair until 4 February, the day after she sailed from Bombay for Aden. When she was only eight hours and 220 miles out from the Indian port, problems arose with the thrust bearings and she was forced to return to Bombay at reduced speed. Although repair parties worked round the clock, it was 11.30 am on 7 February before she could sail again. She had been due to arrive at Tilbury on 19 February, but it was obvious that this could not be met and her call at Aden was cancelled, with three Aden-bound passengers being disembarked and transferred to the *Chusan* which was also sailing that day. In the event the *Arcadia* arrived in London only three days late.

That summer both vessels cruised from Southampton, as they had done since 1954, and many passengers still retain happy memories of those times. Mrs Margaret Eamer of Exeter recalls her first cruise: 'On 17 August 1963 my husband and I joined the *Iberia* for our first ever cruise and there were, in those days, 16 days of bliss for £86. There was no ballroom, just deck space surrounded by fairy lights

The *Iberia* alongside Southampton's 38/39 berth.

(Maritime Photo Library)

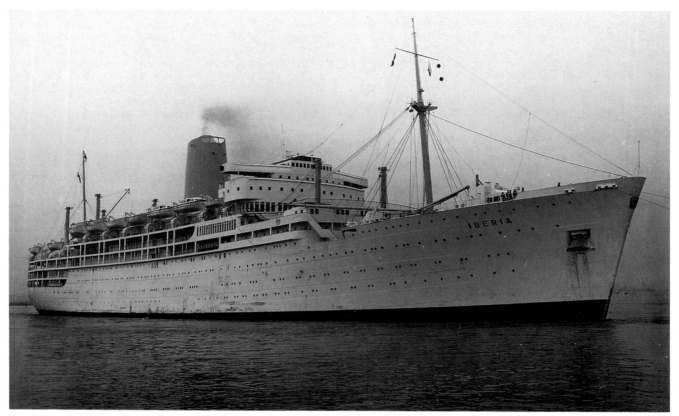

The *Iberia* in Southampton Water.

(F. R. Sherlock)

and a jolly good band. Likewise, there was no cinema, again they used deck space with a portable screen and the audience sat either side of it. We watched Cliff Richard's film "Summer Holiday" back to front and didn't realize it until a sign was reflected in a mirror. It was the same for race night — under the stars on a balmy evening. The only problem I can remember was funnel soot on the after deck and we challenged Captain John Wacher about it. He took it in good part and promptly lay flat out on the deck in this "whites", but he let us have our clothes laundered free. We were leaning on the rail one day, chatting to the Master-At-Arms and watching Stromboli as we passed by when, suddenly, he realized that he could see the sea-bed. "I know the captain hasn't seen Stromboli", he said, "but we aren't planning to go ashore." I can only speak for the tourist class passengers. In those days passengers in the first class were a different breed of person. We did not mix and it always seemed very muted in the first class section. They didn't seem to enjoy themselves as much as we did.'

In April 1965 the *Arcadia* was involved in a Suez Canal mishap when, at 9.30 am on Saturday 24 April, during an outward-bound voyage to Australia with 1,198 passengers on board, she ran aground at Km5 just after entering the canal from Port Said. The weather was very bad at the time and with her bow stuck fast in soft mud she was unable to free herself and so tugs were immediately sent to the scene. It was 2 pm that day before they were able to pull her clear and she then returned to Port Said for an inspection, which found her to be undamaged. However, with continuing bad weather, both north and southbound convoys had been delayed and it was 4.30 am the next

day before she could resume her canal transit. She was then able to make up the lost time, and after cruising in the Pacific Ocean she returned to London by way of the Panama Canal to begin her UK cruise season. The passage to Australia was now very much a secondary role for both ships and it was really more of a positioning voyage for their cruises from either Southampton or in the Pacific. The reduction in the numbers of emigrants to the antipodes, together with competition from jet aircraft, was starting to take its toll on the big passenger ships. However, they were still popular with holiday-makers, as Mr Archie MacKenzie of Gourock recalls with his introduction to cruising in the *Arcadia*: 'I sailed on my first cruise in the *Arcadia* and we left Southampton on 29 August 1965. The *Arcadia* was a two-class ship and we called at Mediterranean ports and Casablanca. Everyone seemed to be expecting gales in the Bay of Biscay and after a smooth crossing the mood relaxed, as the "worst" appeared to be over. Unfortunately, as we were crossing the Golfe Du Lion a Force 9 gale blew up which lasted most of the night. At about 4 pm there was an announcement restricting passengers from going out onto the open decks, and so a lot of passengers chose to have an early night, which gave the stewards and waiters an easy evening. Early next morning we arrived at Villefranche, and there is nothing more "magical" than waking up in a P&O cruise ship to find yourself in a new port — with the sun shining. The *Arcadia* steamed through the gale with no problems, she was an excellent ship and I remember her with affection.'

Although they were both popular ships, they would soon face more tough competition in the form of the 'purpose-built' cruise liner.

The *Iberia* leaving Southampton on 4 September 1971, for a one-week cruise to Bergen and Copenhagen. (Don Smith)

The *Iberia* without her lifeboats, laid up at Southampton's 101 berth in May 1972, shortly before she went to the breaker's yard. (B. Moody)

Chapter Nine

Demise Of The *Iberia*

1966 was a troublesome year, not only for P&O, but for the Merchant Service as a whole. In May 1966 a national seamen's strike began, which lasted for 45 days until 1 July. Any vessels which were in, or arrived at, UK ports during the strike lay idle. The *Arcadia* returned to Southampton from a Mediterranean cruise on 2 June and she was then laid up for the duration of the strike, her remaining two cruises being cancelled. On Saturday 18 June, in order to provide more quay space for the unusually large number of liners present, the *Arcadia* was tied up alongside the *Canberra* at 102 berth in the Western Docks. Although it provided an unusual sight for visitors to the port, it had a devastating effect on the company's finances.

As the *Iberia* was cruising in the Pacific at the time, she was not directly affected by the strike, but encountered her own problems in Japan. On Wednesday 8 June 1966 she left Kobe for Yokohama prior to crossing the Pacific to the West Coast of the USA. However, that same day the engineers detected very bad vibration in the starboard main engines and speed was reduced. As the vibration continued to get worse, it was decided to return to Kobe, but on nearing the port further delays were experienced when a violent storm prevented her from entering harbour. It was 10 June before she was able to berth and Mitsubishi engineers were called in to examine the starboard IP turbine. On inspection they found the turbine claw coupling was very heavily scuffed and worn and a pinion needed to be replaced.

Although the liner was able to sail at 10 pm on 12 June, it was thought prudent to retain Mitsubishi's engineers on board so that any excessive vibration on the starboard propeller shaft could be checked. She arrived in Yokohama on 14 June with no further mechanical problems, but four days late.

The *Arcadia* was able to sail again on 3 July 1966 and she made one two-week cruise into the Mediterranean before leaving London for Australia on 28 July, sailing via Suez. She returned to England by way of Panama on 29 October and just over two weeks later she left once more for Sydney with Penang and Singapore added to the list *en route*. After spending the winter months in the Pacific, she left Sydney for London on 17 February 1967 and returned by way of Manila, Hong Kong, Singapore and Penang, before calling at Bombay and Aden. She made her last transit of the Suez Canal on 17 March, three months before the Arab-Israeli 'Six-Day War' closed the waterway once again — this time for a duration of eight years.

Meanwhile, the *Iberia* had left London on 19 January 1967 for Sydney, sailing by way of the Atlantic and the Panama Canal. Whilst berthing at Funchal, Madeira, she was swinging round when her stem collided with the quayside, tearing the bow plates and bending them to starboard about 8ft above the water-line. After having inspected the damage, the surveyor recommended that a cement box be fitted over the damaged area, and this was completed in time for her to sail at 8.30 pm that day. In the following year she was again

A close-up view of the *Arcadia* and *Canberra* together at 102 berth in June 1966.

(P&O)

Southampton's Western Docks on Saturday 18 June 1966. The *Arcadia* is tied up alongside the *Canberra* at 102 berth. Forward of them are the Union Castle ships *Edinburgh Castle*, *Reina del Mar* and the *Good Hope Castle*. Aft at 104 berth is the *Vaal* and at 106 berth the *Queen Elizabeth* is being manoeuvred alongside.
(Southampton City Museums)

delayed at Funchal when she was on a cruise from Southampton in late September. The voyage had taken her to Lisbon, Alicante, Gibraltar and Las Palmas, with Madeira as the final port of call. However, soon after she arrived there was a complete power failure on board and the boiler feed-water was found to be contaminated. The cause of the problem appeared to be the fresh water evaporators, and with facilities on board greatly reduced it was decided to disembark the passengers into hotels ashore. In the meantime the engineers opened all the evaporator shells and disclosed heavy scale deposits, but the main culprit appeared to be No. 3 evaporator which, as well as being heavily scaled, had 20 badly corroded coils. By working 24-hour shifts all the coils were replaced, and after satisfactory steam tests the *Iberia* was able to re-embark her passengers and sail at 8 am on 4 October 1968. She arrived at 106 berth in Southampton Docks on Monday 7 October and left the following day on her next cruise which had to be cut short by two days.

By now, although she was only 14 years old, the mechanical reliability of the *Iberia* was causing some concern and it was not long before more problems were encountered. On 13 November 1968 she left London for Sydney and after calling at Rotterdam she set courses for Dakar and Cape Town. Three days out, the No. 2 boiler-room forced-draught fan failed, and on her arrival at Dakar it was found that the white metal bearings had melted and an armature shaft was bent. Repairs were carried out successfully by the ship's staff and she was able to leave the port the next day, 24 hours late.

In 1969 P&O decided to use Southampton, instead of Tilbury, as its terminal port, which made good sense because it saved a day's journey up the English Channel. The *Iberia* made her final sailing from Tilbury on 12 June that year, when she left for Southampton and a 14-day cruise. Six months later, on Wednesday 10 December 1969, the *Iberia* 'limped' back into Southampton at the end of a seven-week voyage from Australia which had been plagued by mechanical problems. She had left Sydney on 25 October and after calling at Auckland and Suva her next stop was Pago Pago in Samoa. However, shortly before she arrived there the funnel caught fire and red-hot soot rained down on the deck for 15 minutes. It was thought that the cause had been a leakage of lubricating oil from the burst cover of the No. 2 forced-draught fan. On examination it was found that thousands of feet of wiring needed to be replaced, but as she was considered still seaworthy the voyage was continued. The next problem occurred between Pago Pago and Honolulu, when an electrical failure in the engine-room caused a 24-hour delay. Then after calling at Vancouver, San Francisco and Los Angeles she reached Acapulco, where the starboard main engine failed, which meant that the remainder of the voyage had to be completed at the reduced speed of 19 knots. Even more trouble lay ahead when she called at Curacao in order to refuel. Whilst this operation was under way there was a leak in an oil pipe in the first class baggage room and 170 of the passengers' trunks and cases were covered in thick, black furnace fuel oil. Finally, in view of the vessel's reduced speed, it was decided to cancel a planned call at Cherbourg and sail direct to Southampton after leaving Lisbon on 7 December. It had been a 'jinxed' voyage and on her return she went straight into dry dock for a thorough overhaul. It was during this three-week refit that her mainmast was removed, a modification which certainly suited her.

On completion of the overhaul the *Iberia* sailed once again for Australia via Dakar and Cape Town, and the next two years were remarkably free of trouble. After leaving Southampton on 23 December 1969 she was away for some six months, returning on 8 June 1970. Her summer season from Southampton that year consisted of only two cruises, the first to the Fjords and the second being a three-week voyage into the Mediterranean. Upon her return in late August she left once more for Sydney, again via the west coast of Africa and Cape Town. It was February 1971 before she returned to Southampton and she then steamed round to Rotterdam where

A fine aerial view of the *Iberia* taken in December 1969, after the removal of her mainmast.   *(FotoFlite)*

The *Iberia* in Grand Harbour, Malta, on 1 August 1970 during a Mediterranean cruise. *(M. Cassar)*

she was given a two-week refit before sailing for Sydney and the Pacific. It was to be her last full year of service and upon her return to Southampton in early August she made three cruises from the port.

It was in 1971 that the competition from the jet airliners for the carriage of passengers to all parts of the globe was finally won, when the Boeing 747 'Jumbo' jet entered service. The only alternative for the large passenger ships was cruising and P&O's fleet had adapted well to the new role, but with nine big passenger ships to operate there were far more berths than could be sold to holiday-makers. It was estimated that P&O's ships were making their line voyages to Australia only 60 to 70 per cent full, with this figure increasing by only 10 per cent on cruises. In addition, the continued closure of the Suez Canal meant longer voyages and increased operating costs. In 1972 P&O bought the still uncompleted *Spirit of London,* which was being built in Italy, and with delivery due for October that year it was clear that the purpose-built cruise ships were going to be the way ahead.

The *Iberia* made her last line sailing from Southampton on 6 November 1971, after having spent six weeks in the port, and she arrived in Sydney, via Panama, on 22 December to start her cruise season based in the port. However, after only two cruises, it came as no real surprise when P&O announced on 3 February 1972 that on completion of her Australian cruise programme, the *Iberia* was to be withdrawn from service and sold. At the same time P&O began to switch more of their tonnage from line voyages, of which there were to be only four a year, to cruising. Of the *Iberia* a P&O spokesman said: 'The main trouble with the *Iberia* is that she has been getting more than usually heavier with age.' It was an oblique reference to

her machinery problems, her lack of stability and her relatively short range of operation.

After making three more cruises from Sydney, the *Iberia* left the port for the last time on 16 March 1972, commanded by Captain Maurice A. Trenfield and bound for Southampton. She made the voyage by way of the south Australian ports, then Fremantle, Durban, Cape Town, Dakar, Lisbon and Vigo, arriving at 105 berth in Southampton on Wednesday 19 April 1972, with an 18ft paying-off pennant flying from her mast. Captain Trenfield rang 'finished with engines' and left the ship for a well-earned retirement. At the end of April the *Iberia* was laid up at 101 berth to await a buyer.

That month P&O announced the withdrawal of three more ships, the *Chusan, Orcades* and *Oronsay,* during a painful period of restructuring for the company's passenger fleet, and it was clear that these ships were destined for the scrapyard. In mid-June 1972 it was disclosed that the *Iberia* had been sold to shipbreakers in Taiwan and that she would leave the port for her delivery voyage on Tuesday 28 June.

The sad task of taking her to the scrapyard fell to Captain Michael Prowse and 66 crew members — 14 on deck, 20 in the engine-room and 32 catering and fire-patrol staff. The liner made the voyage under a cargo ship certificate and she slipped from Southampton almost unnoticed on the appointed day. There were no streamers, no passengers and she carried only two lifeboats, one on either side. She made calls for fuel at Dakar, Durban, Mauritius and Hong Kong, finally arriving at Kaohsiung on 5 September 1972. She was just 18 years old.

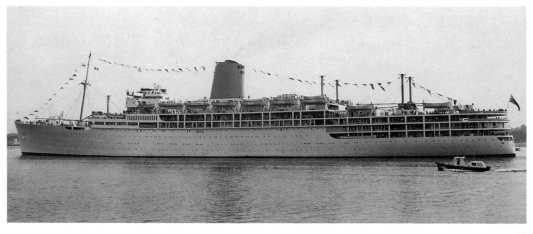

The *Iberia* leaves Southampton for a cruise in the summer of 1972.

(A. Duncan)

Chapter Ten

Arcadia Meets The Challenge

Unlike the *Iberia,* the *Arcadia* had always been a reliable vessel and she also had a reputation for being a happy ship and, since her early days under Captain Forrest, her ship's company had always kept a team spirit alive. All these qualities would be required to keep the *Arcadia* at sea during the late 1960s and into the 1970s in the highly competitive cruise market.

In 1969, with the withdrawal of P&O from Tilbury, Southampton became the *Arcadia's* terminal port, which it always had been during the summer cruising season, and she made her first line voyage out of the port on 14 November that year. She sailed via Las Palmas and Cape Town, arriving in Sydney on 18 December. She then spent several weeks cruising on long voyages usually to the US West Coast, and in early March 1970 she set out once again for Southampton via Cape Town, arriving back just over four weeks later on 6 April. During her three-week stay in the port she underwent a refit by Thorneycroft's, which included removing her mainmast and shortening the foremast by about 18 feet. These modifications were necessary to enable her to clear low-hanging power cables in Alaskan waters where she was soon to be employed. On completion of the overhaul, the *Arcadia* left Southampton bound for Panama via Cherbourg, Bermuda and Port Everglades, before going on to Vancouver. She spent the next five months cruising from San Francisco and Vancouver, on seven- and 14-day cruises, but she did not venture north to Alaska during this season.

She returned to Southampton in September 1970 to make three autumn cruises to the Mediterranean before leaving for Cape Town and Sydney in mid-November. There she repeated the pattern of the previous year, making three long cruises before returning to

Southampton by way of South Africa, in April 1971. After a short refit she returned to North America, where she remained until July that year before returning home via Sydney, Singapore and South Africa. During the early 1970s she spent very little time in UK waters, but upon her return to Southampton from Vancouver in June 1972, and whilst her sister ship *Iberia* lay at 107 berth awaiting departure to the shipbreaker's yard, she was chosen to host the P&O Pensioners' reunion luncheon. During the meeting Mr Peter Parry, the Chief Executive of the company's Passenger Division, confirmed that following the withdrawal of the *Iberia, Chusan, Orcades* and *Oronsay,* the remaining vessels would be employed mainly on cruising; the traditional trading routes were to be abandoned. It was also made clear that the main thrust of the new cruise market was to be in North America.

That summer the *Arcadia* made only two cruises from Southampton before returning to Sydney, and she came back to her home port only once that year for her annual refit in December. It was during this overhaul that she was converted to an open-class ship in preparation for her changed role. She was to be away from UK waters for the whole of 1973, making a series of cruises along the West Coast of the USA and Canada, as well as three 28-day Caribbean cruises and two 16-day Hawaiian cruises. She now had accommodation for 1,350 passengers, the large, six-berth cabins on F Deck having been retained. The former first class dining saloon's name was changed from the Olympic to the Cotswold Restaurant, and the ex-tourist class Corinthian became the Plymouth Restaurant. All the other names of public rooms with an 'Arcadian' theme were also changed. The Observation Lounge became The Lookout, the writing rooms at

The *Arcadia,* her mainmast having been removed, passes beneath Vancouver's Lions Gate Bridge. *(A. Duncan)*

During July 1972 the *Arcadia* ventured north to Alaskan waters. Here she is seen in Glacier Bay. *(Jalcruise Overseas Ltd.)*

Another view of the *Arcadia* in Glacier Bay. *(Jalcruise Overseas Ltd.)*

the forward end of the Promenade Deck became the Shelley Room and Hardy Room, and the first class lounge was renamed the Devon Room. Further aft, the Verandah Café became the Dorchester Room and the ex-tourist class lounge the Cornwall Room, whilst the Smoking Room just aft again became the Raleigh Room. Aft on B Deck the former tourist class dance space and Verandah Café were renamed the Rose & Crown and Drake's Tavern respectively.

The *Arcadia* left Southampton on 22 December 1972 and it was to be nearly two and a half years before she returned. During her time on the US West Coast in 1973, Captain Anthony Dallas made a 'whistle-stop' tour of Arizona, California and Oregon to 'sell' cruises and voyages aboard the *Arcadia,* for everything possible had to be done to keep the ship in service. Captain Joe Chapman recalls his command of the *Arcadia* at this time: 'I took command of *Arcadia* in San Francisco on 6 July 1973, immediately prior to her first long Pacific cruise. Our first port of call after leaving Vancouver was Anchorage, in Alaska, and it was the first time that a P&O vessel had sailed that far north in the Pacific. Our visit to Glacier Bay was marred by damp and hazy weather, but with the help of the pilot — aptly named Dan Starkweather — we reached Lampling Glacier where we lowered a boat to collect ice for the champagne which was served at the buffet lunch. The pilots for Anchorage boarded at Homer late on the brilliantly clear evening of 13 July and *Arcadia* docked there the following morning, 14 July. The enormous tidal range caused some concern with gangways and at low water a brow was run from the wharf to the Promenade Deck.

We sailed from Anchorage in the early evening and, in view of a forecast indicating dense fog over the entire area south of the Aleutians, I decided to go into the Bering Sea, which we entered at noon on 16 July by way of the Unimak Pass. Any more than 24 hours steaming north of the Aleutians would have increased the distance to Yokohama so I had to face the fog and we left the Bering Sea on the morning of 17 July, by the Adak Strait. Dense fog persisted

for the following two days, but we berthed at Yokohama on time.

The remainder of the voyage was enjoyed in fine weather, the only disappointment being the need to cancel a planned visit to Nuku Hiva in the Marquesas Islands, due to the withdrawal of fuel oil supplies at Papeete. This was essential if we were to add distance with a call at Nuku Hiva.'

In November and December 1973, after another long Pacific and East Asian cruise from San Francisco, instead of returning to Southampton for her annual refit, the work was carried out by Yarrows at their picturesque Esquimalt yard, the same shipyard which had converted the P&O liner *Rajputana* for service as an armed merchant cruiser in the early weeks of the Second World War.

In October 1974, with the withdrawal of the *Himalaya* from the Australian cruise market, and the introduction of P&O Princess Cruises on the US West Coast, the *Arcadia* was transferred to Sydney where she made a series of short cruises based on the port. She was now in her 21st year of service, which in the economic climate of those days was no mean feat, but it was clear that there would not be too many more anniversary celebrations for her. The competition now was from purpose-built cruise ships, three of which were being operated by P&O themselves by the end of 1974.

The *Arcadia* returned to Southampton at 1 pm on Friday 21 March 1975 after an absence of over two years, but her renewed acquaintance with the port was to be short-lived for she was scheduled to sail for Sydney once again on 17 May. After a three-week refit by Vosper-Thorneycroft, she left on a 14-day cruise to the Atlantic Isles, followed by an unusual four-day cruise to Amsterdam and back, with fares in a six-berth cabin starting at £44. Her positioning cruise to Sydney in May and June that year took her down the west coast of Africa via Cape Town and Durban and it was, in fact, the last time she would visit South Africa. The next eight months were spent making short cruises to Pacific ports, and longer cruises to Asian destinations.

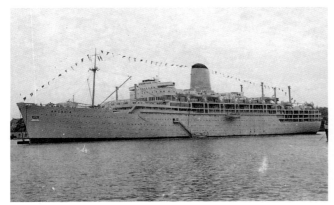

The *Arcadia* at Malta in October 1970. *(M. Cassar)*

The *Arcadia* passes Sydney Heads. *(M. Cassar)*

Arcadia in Canadian Waters. *(J. K. Byass)*

The *Arcadia* at Lisbon in May 1975. The way her forward mast has been shortened can be seen to good effect. *(E. H. Cole)*

Chapter Eleven

The End For The *Arcadia*

On her return to Australia the *Arcadia* continued to cruise from Sydney, where she was always a firm favourite. In 1977, when the liner was not included in P&O's UK cruise programme, there was some speculation as to her future, but P&O made reassuring noises. However, in the P&O Group's annual report for that year the poor economic climate in Australia was highlighted, and in his statement the chairman announced that the devaluation of the Australian dollar in 1976 had severely depressed the earnings from *Arcadia's* early 1977 cruises. He went on to say that although the situation had improved, these conditions had had a disastrous effect on the liner's profitability. Seen against this background the future looked bleak, and by the summer of 1978 P&O were seriously considering what to do about their 24-year-old passenger vessel. She had been built to carry both passengers and cargo on the service to Australia, and her upper decks were cluttered with hatches, kingposts and all the machinery and equipment required for cargo handling. Therefore it came as no real surprise when, in September that year, P&O announced that they had purchased the 26,600-ton, ex-Swedish-America Line ship *Kungsholm* and that, after a conversion refit, she would replace the *Arcadia* in the Australian cruise market. She had been completed in 1966 and had accommodation for just 450 passengers in far more comfortable surroundings than the *Arcadia* could offer. The conversion of the vessel was carried out in Germany and the resulting appearance, according to P&O, showed a profile similar to their three ships in the Princess Cruises fleet. However, many people thought that the lines of a truly lovely vessel had been spoiled by the rebuilding. In keeping with their new naming policy, P&O renamed the ship *Sea Princess,* although she took on the traditional white livery and a buff funnel. The completion of the conversion work was delayed by a few weeks due to unusually severe weather conditions, but in late January 1979 she left Germany for Singapore where she was scheduled to replace the *Arcadia.*

Meanwhile, in Sydney on 29 January 1979, 25 years after P&O had taken delivery of her, the *Arcadia* left the port on her final cruise. It was a most unusual voyage which had been marketed as a '36-day Eastern Adventure' during which her passengers would call at Brisbane, Rabaul, Hong Kong and Singapore. There they had the opportunity to 'ring out the old and ring in the new' as they were transferred to the *Sea Princess* to continue the voyage.

The *Arcadia's* last day in Sydney had been a busy one as she disembarked 1,250 passengers and then embarked her last

A fine aerial view of the *Arcadia* at sea in the 1970s and how most people would wish to remember her.　　　(*FotoFlite*)

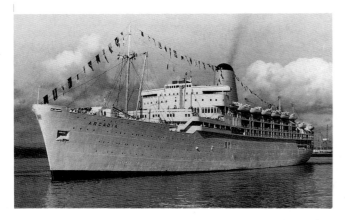

The *Arcadia* leaves Southampton in April 1976 for one of her last cruises from the port. *(F. R. Sherlock)*

holiday-makers. It was a public holiday on Monday 29 January, as Australians celebrated the arrival of the first fleet in 1788, and huge crowds turned out to see the *Arcadia* steam slowly out of the harbour. A pipe band played 'Scotland the Brave', recalling her Clydebank origins, and thousands of streamers stretched in a colourful kaleidoscope before snapping as the last links with Australia were broken. As the *Arcadia* sailed regally towards the Heads, she was escorted by scores of small craft, including fireboats and even an old steam yacht. The air resounded to a cacophony of ships' whistles and car horns and many of those watching the old ship, dressed overall and with her 25-ft paying off pennant flying proudly, must have recalled their first glimpses of Australia from the *Arcadia's* decks, or happy holidays in the sun.

Her master, Captain Anthony Dallas, when asked in a media interview about his feelings said: 'My first thoughts, as always, will be for the safety of the ship, but if there is a spare moment I shall feel sad, sad that this beautiful ship has come to the end of her days.'

For the *Arcadia* the cruise ended in Singapore on 21 February 1979, when her passengers and a large number of her crew members transferred to the *Sea Princess*. Captain Dallas then had the task of delivering the *Arcadia* to the shipbreaker's in Taiwan to whom she had been sold. She arrived in Kaohsiung on 27 February where, because her scheduled breaking berth was not available, she was tied up alongside a Greek oil-tanker which was awaiting the same fate.

One of the last people to travel in, and to witness the *Arcadia's* final humiliation, was the American author and businessman James L. Shaw. Here Jim recalls his unique experiences: 'The last voyage, I found, was already booked solid but I had my name down, just in case something came up — even though I couldn't afford it. Two weeks later, however, a letter arrived from P&O Australia stating that "on receipt of Aust $429" I would be booked into cabin 263 on E Deck for the final voyage to Hong Kong. Three months, 12 short days and many dollars later the trip was over. The *Arcadia* had berthed at Hong Kong's Ocean Terminal and was now waiting to proceed to Singapore to meet an overdue *Sea Princess*. The trip from Sydney had shown that her hull was still sound and her engines strong — she made 21 knots for most of the journey. The plumbing and electrical fittings were showing their age, with some even held on with twine, but even that could not detract from the final voyage of a ship which had played a part in the lives of so many.'

As the *Arcadia* was destined for Taiwan Jim Shaw visited the shipbreaker's on 6 and 7 March, only seven days after her arrival there: 'A business acquaintance in Kaohsiung agreed to meet me at the airport and act as my guide through the breaking yards. To see the dismantlers at work Mr Wang suggested that we seek out the *Arcadia* and this meant a drive over to the Dah Lin Pu yards where she had been tied up. At a small fishing pier we were greeted by a

Looking deserted and utterly forlorn. The *Arcadia* at the breaker's yard in Kaohsiung on 6 March 1979. She had been given a list to starboard so that her remaining fuel oil could be recovered. *(J. L. Shaw)*

lifeboat full of furniture from the *Arcadia*, the dismantling process had already begun. Mr Wang talked briefly with the Chinese lady in command of the boat and we were soon being whisked off to the *Arcadia*. The picture was bleak. The *Arcadia* had been given a list to starboard so that the remaining fuel oil could be recovered and it was being pumped into several of the ship's own lifeboats for transportation ashore. Above us furniture and mattresses were being lifted over the rails and lowered down into waiting boats. Most of these items would be sold in second-hand stores to restaurants and shops.

We climbed up the pilot's ladder and into a companion-way situated on the *Arcadia's* lower decks. A guard listened patiently and then waved us into the dark interior. There was no electricity or lights and the ship was silent and dead, the only noise to be heard was a single cylinder pump working on the oil supply far below. Our flashlights caught cabin numbers which all appeared to be closed and locked, ahead of us on the main staircase dark forms were moving bundles of bedding. I came across the cabin which I had occupied for the final voyage — the door was closed, but it was not locked. Inside the contents were intact, only the bedding was missing. At the sink two glasses still stood in their holders, two towels still hung on their hooks and the orange life-jackets still overflowed from the closets. Nothing had been disturbed.

We continued on up the main staircase and on A Deck there was

The swimming-pool on the Promenade Deck. Compare this desolate scene with the view in Chapter Three. *(J. L. Shaw)*

enough natural light by which to see. On the Promenade Deck workers had just finished rolling up sections of carpet in the Devon and Camelot Rooms and overhead lights had been torn from their fixtures. Most of the furniture had already disappeared over the side of the ship. Forward in one of the small reading rooms we came across Mr Ming H. Wu of Rainbow Enterprises. He was an antique dealer and he had purchased most of the *Arcadia's* decorative furnishings and brass. He now had the Hardy Room stacked full and

'One deck up a solitary worker was removing the large glass wind-breaks which, at sea, had constantly vibrated and "chattered." Everywhere the gallant old ship was coming apart.' *(J. L. Shaw)*

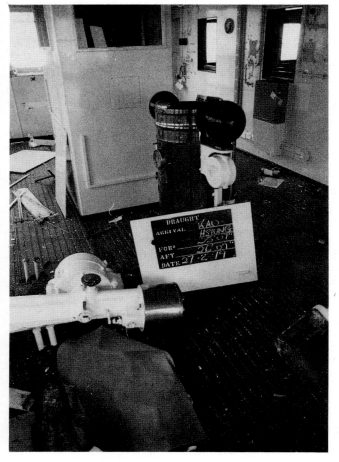

The *Arcadia's* chartroom was a shambles, but the board recording her draught on arrival at Kaohsiung on 27 February 1979 can be seen. *(J. L. Shaw)*

he was taking an inventory of his collection.

Going out on deck we found more workers busily chiselling up the *Arcadia's* hardwood decks and assembling it in bundles for transportation ashore. One deck up a solitary worker was methodically removing the large glass wind-breaks which, at sea, had constantly vibrated and "chattered". Everywhere the gallant old ship was coming apart.

One last pinnacle required my inspection — the navigating bridge. We went forward to the main staircase, passing the Lookout Bar. It was a shambles. The carpet had been ripped up and the drapes pulled down. Bare wires dangled from the ceiling and furniture was lying about. It had been my favourite place to enjoy a drink before dinner,

now it was being destroyed. The officers' quarters and the captain's cabin had been ransacked, the debris was strewn everywhere. On the bridge itself the scenes were repeated — it was a sorry sight after having witnessed the attentive care which the crew had given to daily maintenance.

I had seen enough. The *Arcadia* was only a machine, but it seemed a disgrace to tear apart such a lovely creation. We made our way back down the *Arcadia's* darkened passageways to the embarkation ladder.'

A few months later one of her ex-radio officers visited the yard at Kaohsiung and found only the foremast and 200 feet of hull left. Soon afterwards the *Arcadia* ceased to exist.

In the Dorchester Room the carpets have been rolled up and the decorative panel which represented the chart of the world has gone. This was once the first class Verandah Café, shown in happier times in Chapter Three. *(J. L. Shaw)*

The dismantling of the *Arcadia* is well under way and the cutting torches have almost reached her funnel. *(J. L. Shaw)*

Principal Particulars

	Arcadia	*Iberia*
Length Overall	718ft 9in	718ft 9in
Length b.p.	668ft	668ft
Breadth moulded	90ft 6in	90ft 6in
Load draught	31ft	31ft
Gross tonnage	29,734	29,500
Net tonnage	16,077	15,885
Passengers:		
First class	679	674
Tourist class	735	733
One class	1,350	N/A
Crew	711	711
General cargo	211,000 cu ft	157,180 cu ft
Insulated cargo	158,500 cu ft	147,750 cu ft
SHP	34,000 both ships	
Service speed	22.5 knots both ships	

Other titles from FAN PUBLICATIONS:

Canberra & Sea Princess £6.95

Famous British Liners:
Vol. 1 *SS Oriana* — The Last Great Orient Liner £6.95
Vol 2 *SS Viceroy of India* — P&O's First Electric Cruise Liner £6.95

Write for further details to
FAN PUBLICATIONS, 17 Wymans Lane, Cheltenham, Glos, GL51 9QA, England.

Acknowledgements

Mr Don Smith for permission to use his colour transparencies. Readers wishing to purchase copy slides should write to Mr Smith at 7 Chapel Court, Hambleton, Selby, Yorkshire, YO8 9YF.

Ian Spashett, FotoFlite for permission to use photographs from the company's collection. Readers wishing to purchase these photographs should contact FotoFlite, Littlestone Road, New Romney, Kent, TN28 8NP.

James L. Shaw of Milwaukie, Oregon, USA, for permission to use his very poignant photographs of the *Arcadia* at the breaker's yard and his memories of her final voyage.

Thanks to Claire Hider, Katy Morgan, Lyn Palmer, Norman W. Pound, of the P&O Company, London.

R. R. (Bob) Aspinall, Museum of London: A. E. Bell, Cookham, Berkshire: J. Blackburn, Alton, Hampshire: Mrs E. J. Booth, Frimley, Surrey: M. Cassar, Valletta, Malta: D. Chambers, Kinross, Tayside: Captain J. L. Chapman RD, RNR, (Rtd.), Truro, Cornwall: Mrs S. Coulson, Benfleet, Essex: Father D. Drake-Brockman, Leeds, Yorkshire: Margaret Dykes, Doncaster, South Yorkshire: A. Duncan, Gravesend, Kent: A. Dyson, Burnley, Lancashire: Margaret Eamer, Exeter, Devon: Mrs Margaret Hodge, MBE, Roehampton, London: D. D. Hughes, Durban, South Africa: A. MacKenzie, Gourock, Scotland: M. J. Miles, Diss, Norfolk: B. Moody, Southampton: I. Morris, Southampton: D. J. Orchard, Victoria, Australia: C. Parsons, Manchester: P. R. Salisbury, Weston-Super-Mare, Avon: Captain C. R. Short, Chester: D. Smedley, Potters Bar, Hertfordshire: Rachel Smith, Southampton City Museums: Finally to my wife Freda and my two daughters Caroline & Louise.

The *Iberia* at Sydney.

(Captain J. L. Chapman)

The *Iberia* at Southampton.

(P&O)

The *Arcadia* leaving Tilbury in the early 1960s.   *(D. Chambers)*

The *Arcadia* at sea.   *(P&O)*